THE
GRILLING
BIBLE

Publications International, Ltd.

Favorite Brand Name Recipes at www.fbnr.com

Some of the products listed in this publication may be in limited distribution.

Contributing Writer: Marilyn Pocius

Pictured on the front cover *(counterclockwise from top left):* Backyard Barbecue Burger *(page 50),* Jamaican Baby Back Ribs *(page 160)* and Classic Grilled Chicken *(page 52).*
Pictured on the back cover *(clockwise from center right):* Grilled Coriander Corn *(page 234),* Asian Grilled Steak with Spicy Herb Sauce *(page 84)* and Carolina-Style Barbecue Chicken *(page 116).*

ISBN-13: 978-1-4127-2155-4
ISBN-10: 1-4127-2155-5

Library of Congress Control Number: 2004113594

Manufactured in China.

8 7 6 5 4 3 2 1

Microwave Cooking: Microwave ovens vary in wattage. Use the cooking times as guidelines and check for doneness before adding more time.

Preparation/Cooking Times: Preparation times are based on the approximate amount of time required to assemble the recipe before cooking, baking, chilling or serving. These times include preparation steps such as measuring, chopping and mixing. The fact that some preparations and cooking can be done simultaneously is taken into account. Preparation of optional ingredients and serving suggestions is not included.

Contents

The Joy of Cooking Outdoors

What is it about grilling that so captures the American imagination? Is it cooking in the wide open spaces and the great outdoors? Or is it the primitive delight of playing with fire? Maybe it's just how good food tastes when it's kissed with smoke and seared to perfection.

Holding meat on a stick over a fire is certainly the first cooking method devised by humans. We've come a long way since with our fancy gas grills, custom-made utensils, national barbecue contests and vehement opinions on the subject. Still, the basics haven't truly changed. The chemistry of food over fire is a simple and delicious one. Grilling really is one of the easiest and quickest ways to make natural flavors shine. From a toasted marshmallow to a slightly charred t-bone steak, everything from the grill just plain tastes better.

The Grilling Bible is a resource for those who are just learning to light a fire and expert flame-tenders alike. For those just getting started, there is help choosing the right grill and understanding terminology such as "indirect heat" and "wet rub." For the more experienced practitioner, there's advice on grilling a whole fish or a pizza perfectly.

Over 190 recipes will tempt you to fire up the grill for parties, for quick weeknight dinners and, if you're like some dedicated barbecue aficionados, even when you have to brush the snow off the grill to get started. It won't be long before you're adding grill marks to everything from tuna to tomatoes. So come on outside and light that fire! Grilling makes any other kind of cooking seem way too tame.

Choosing a Grill

Before you run off to the local hardware store or home center to face all the options—Btu, lava rocks, side burners, smoking boxes—take some time to decide what kind of grilling you want to do. The first choice you face is charcoal or gas.

Charcoal grills generally burn hotter than gas grills. They're easier to use for smoking and there are those who claim that charcoal is the only way to get authentic grilled flavor. (There are also studies that claim to prove the difference in flavor between charcoal and gas grilled food is undetectable.) A charcoal grill does gives you more opportunity to indulge the primal urge to play with fire.

Gas grills light instantly with the push of a button and offer steady heat that is easily adjusted. They make it easier to grill anything at anytime. Chances are you're not going to go to the trouble of lighting charcoal to make

Is your grilling personality better suited to charcoal or gas?

Check the statements that sound most like you.

A. Getting someplace is half the fun. I like to take my time and do it right.

B. I consider myself an efficient person. If something can be done quicker and easier, I'm all for it.

A. I'm into traditional cooking methods. I want to experiment with smoking, slow-cooking and the flavor different kinds of wood can give grilled food.

B. I'm likely to decide what I'm cooking for dinner on the way home from work.

A. I'm a back-to-nature kind of person. Part of the joy of grilling is being outdoors.

B. I want to be able to easily grill anything anytime, even in the dead of winter.

A. Grilling is more than a way to cook. It's about lazy summer weekends and inviting folks over to share food and friendship.

B. I love to throw spontaneous parties. "Bring a salad and come over. I'll throw something on the grill."

If you chose more "A" answers, you're grilling personality leans towards charcoal; mostly "B" means you'd likely be happier with a gas grill.

hot dogs on a Monday night. With a gas grill, it's a snap. There are, of course, some people who own and use both charcoal and gas grills.

The bottom line is that either charcoal or gas will do an excellent job. Here are some tips on buying a grill that will be a joy to use for many years.

What to Look for in All Grills

Overall Construction: A sturdy, long-lasting grill is heavy and made of high-grade steel rather than aluminum. Just lifting the cover should tell you a lot. Is it heavy? Does it fit tightly? The finish should be baked-on porcelain-enamel, not just sprayed-on paint. Legs should be welded on. Wheels should be heavy-duty.

Brand Name: Buying a familiar brand name with a reputation for quality is a good bet. Check the warranty period (usually a 5-year limited warranty for charcoal and 10 years for gas) to see if the manufacturer stands behind the product. If you're planning to live with a grill for many seasons, you'll also want to be able to replace grids and other parts, which is easier if they're stocked at your local hardware store.

Cooking Grids (Grates): Look for grids made of nickel-plated or porcelain-coated cast iron for

maximum heat retention, ease of cleaning and rust resistance. Uncoated stainless steel grids resist rust but may allow food to stick. Uncoated cast iron grids retain heat well, but will require frequent seasoning.

Capacity: Bigger is not necessarily better. If you will only be cooking for two, you don't want to waste fuel heating up a giant grill every time you crave a burger. Consider clearance when the grill is covered, too. If it's important to you to be able to grill a 16 pound turkey, it needs to fit comfortably under the grill cover. It's also helpful to measure the area where you're planning to place the grill in your backyard. There should be enough room to keep it away from your deck, house and even shrubs. Judging size in the store can be deceiving, so think ahead.

Thermometer: It's convenient to have a thermometer that registers the temperature inside a grill that can be read from outside. Opening a grill to check the temperature lowers it drastically and adds to cooking times.

Cost: Grills range from cheap portable models up to super-sized stainless behemoths that attach to a permanent gas line. Obviously, prices rise with size and features. Gas grills cost more than charcoal grills to buy, but overall you'll spend less on fuel with a gas grill. As with most products, choosing solely on price is not a good idea. A cheap grill will often be frustrating to use and it can rust out in a single season.

Charcoal Grills: Features to Look For

Air Vents: To control temperatures, you'll need to open and close vents to adjust the oxygen supply. There should be vents both underneath the charcoal chamber and in the lid.

Ash Catcher: Most charcoal grills have a device that will sweep used ashes into a disposal pan of some type. It often works by sliding the vent lever back and forth to knock the ashes through the vent holes in the bottom. It helps if the disposal pan can be removed to dump the cooled ashes.

Side Baskets: This feature makes it easy to cook over indirect heat because it holds the coals on each side of the grill, making it simple to place a drip pan in the center. If a grill doesn't come with side baskets, you can often buy them to add on later.

Hinged Grid/Grate: A handy feature that allows you to lift the grid and add more coals or wood to the fire without removing the food. It's especially helpful if you'll be doing a lot of long, slow barbecuing.

Optional Goodies: Side tables, utensil holders and rotisserie attachments are available. Some manufacturers are now creating grills with built-in chimney charcoal starters.

Gas Grills: Features to Look For

Burners: You'll need two at the very least. Three or four burners are even better. This allows you to turn off a burner(s) and grill over indirect or low heat. (See page 16 for explanations of indirect heat.)

Cooking System: The familiar smoky flavor of charcoal grilling comes from food juices dripping onto hot charcoal and being vaporized. Gas grills produce the same effect with lava rocks, ceramic briquets or metal heat plates or bars.

- Lava rocks heat quickly, but are porous so they allow grease to accumulate. This lessens efficiency and increases the chances for flare-ups. For these reasons lava rocks must usually be replaced yearly.

- Ceramic briquets stay clean longer than lava rocks since they don't absorb grease and residue is burned off more completely.

- Metal heat plates or bars (sometimes called flavorizer bars) vaporize juices fast and don't need to be replaced as often as lava rocks or briquets.

Btu: Btu is short for British thermal unit and while it is a measure of heat output, it can be very misleading. Choosing a grill because it has a bigger Btu number may sound like a good idea, but it's probably not. A grill's cooking temperatures and performance are based on size, construction and grid dimension. Some cooking systems are more efficient than others, so they reach higher temperatures with a lower Btu.

Drip Pan: This device collects grease; it should be easy to empty. Some drip pans hold disposable liners to make clean-up easier.

Gas Gauge: To prevent running out of gas in the middle of cooking a roast or a rack of ribs, look for a grill with a gas gauge.

Optional Goodies: A smoker box holds mesquite or other wood chips; side burners keep barbecue sauce warm. Other options include rotisseries, grill lights, side tables and utensil holders.

Cleaning and Caring for a Grill

Your brand new grill will be shiny and pristine, but it won't stay that way. And that's okay. We've all seen examples of both ends of the cleanliness spectrum: the grill grid that's scrubbed so thoroughly every time it's used it positively gleams; or, the other extreme, the grill that features crusted-on samples of virtually every food ever prepared. Neither extreme is desirable. One of the most important steps in caring for any grill is to read and keep the owner's manual, which will give specific dos and don'ts to keep your investment in good condition.

Every Time You Grill
Cleaning the Cooking Surface

Clean the grid each time you grill so food doesn't stick or pick up flavors from your last cooking session. You don't need abrasives or oven cleaners, just a few minutes of maintenance.

After the grill is preheated and before you cook, rub the grid with a dry, stiff wire brush. You'll need a long-handled one or an oven mitt to protect yourself. The heat not only sterilizes the grid but makes it easier to get off those last few burned-on bits.

When you're through grilling, let the heat do the hard part of the work once again. Let the fire burn on high for 10 minutes or so until any stuck-on food is incinerated. (A self-cleaning oven works the same way, by super heating the interior.) Then brush the grid thoroughly with the same stiff wire brush.

Keeping the grill grid lubricated will also help keep it clean. Oil the grid with cooking oil every time you use it. Use a paper towel or clean rag soaked in cooking oil or a can of spray oil. For best results (and good grill marks), oil the grid when it's hot. If you are using cooking spray, remove the grid from the fire wearing a heavy duty grill glove and hold it a safe distance from the grill before spraying.

Caring for the Firebox

Remove cold ashes from the bottom of a charcoal grill. (A garden trowel is a good tool to use to shovel them out.) This makes it easier to build a new fire and helps prevent rusting since ashes absorb moisture.

Gas grill owners should empty or change the drip pan whenever grease begins to accumulate.

As Needed Maintenance
Charcoal Grills

Oven cleaner may be used on many grids to remove major stuck-on grease deposits. (Check your owner's manual to make sure it's recommended.) Wait until the grid is cold and place it on plenty of newspapers before spraying on the cleaner. Give the oven cleaner the appropriate amount of time and wash it off completely following package directions.

Use a nonabrasive cloth or sponge to clean the rest of the grill. Be sure to dry it off to prevent rusting. You can usually use a soapy, fine steel wool pad to gently scrub problem areas, but be careful not to scratch enameled portions of the grill.

Gas Grills

Clean the bottom tray that is over the drip pan with a scraper or steel brush regularly. (It usually pulls out from

under the grill.) A build up of grease and debris is a fire hazard. Although it may sound like a labor-saving idea to line this pan with foil, it is usually not recommended since creases in the foil can trap grease and cause a fire. It is okay to line the drip pan itself with foil or to use the disposable foil drip-pan liners that are available for many models. Consult your owner's manual to learn the options for your grill.

Use mild soapy water to clean off the exterior of your grill. Using harsh cleansers (especially if they are lemon-based) can damage the finish.

Examine the lava rocks or briquets. If they are cracked or have collected grease and residue, replace them. If your grill utilizes v-bars or other flavorizer bars, brush off any debris with a scraper or wire brush.

Check to see that your burners are heating evenly. There should be blue flames in all the gas outlets across the span of the burners. If any are clogged, you can clean them with a flexible wire or paper clip. If burners are cracked or damaged, replace them. The metal conduits that carry gas to the burners are called venturis. When the grill is not being used venturis often become homes to spiders and insects. Consult your owner's manual to learn how to remove the burner and clean the venturis with a special brush if they become clogged.

A Few Grill Cleaning Don'ts

1. NEVER use wax or ordinary paint on the lid of your grill. If you do need to touch up a chipped surface, purchase specially formulated high-temperature grill paint.

2. NEVER spray cooking oil directly onto the cooking grid of a hot grill without removing it. The droplets of oil can easily catch fire.

3. DON'T attack a porcelain-coated grill grid with scrapers or other harsh cleansers. You could chip the coating. Use a brass-bristled brush and consult your owner's manual for proper cleaning methods.

4. NEVER try to dispose of ashes while they are still hot. NEVER try to clean or put a cover on a hot grill.

5. NEVER use oven cleaner on the painted surfaces of a grill. It can remove paint.

Lighting Your Fire

Fire Hazards

1. NEVER start a fire with gasoline, kerosene, naphtha or paint thinner.

2. Keep cans of lighter fluid far from the fire and NEVER add more lighter fluid to burning coals.

3. NEVER light a chimney starter on a wooden deck or other flammable surface.

4. Open the cover of a gas grill BEFORE turning on the gas.

5. NEVER grill inside, in a tent, under a porch or in any enclosure.

Lighting a Charcoal Grill

In the early days of grilling, the height of the flames leaping out of your grill when you lit it was a point of pride. Not any more—today's griller knows that using too much chemical-based lighter fluid can leave a residue that lingers unpleasantly in the flavor of the cooked food. Fortunately, these days there are better lighter fluids and plenty of other options. However you start your fire, first make sure the vents in the bottom of your grill are open so the fire gets needed oxygen.

Lighter Fluid: If you do use lighter fluid, read and follow the instructions on the package. (Most brands call for waiting to let the fluid penetrate before lighting the charcoal.) Pile the coals in a pyramid, douse them with fluid and light with a long-handled match or wand-type butane lighter. NEVER try to add lighter fluid to coals that are already burning. The fire can follow the stream of lighter fluid back towards your hand and the can with disastrous results.

Self-Lighting Charcoal: These briquets have been impregnated with the right amount of starter fluid so they burn easily and evenly. They're convenient, but your food may still get some of the chemical flavor that comes with lighter fluid.

Chimney Starter: This hollow metal cylinder allows you to light charcoal quickly and evenly without a drop of lighter fluid. Place the chimney starter on the charcoal grate (not the cooking grid) and put crumpled newspaper in the bottom section. Fill the top section with charcoal (or hardwood). Light the newspaper underneath to ignite the coals and wait until they glow orange-red. This process takes 15 to 25 minutes. Wearing a heavy oven mitt

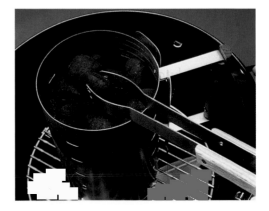

to protect your hand, pick up the starter by the handle, dump the coals into the grill, and you're ready to go.

Electric Starter: This device is a looped heating element on a handle. Snuggle it in among the coals and plug it in. It will glow red and ignite the coals. Wait 10 to 15 minutes until most of the coals are lit before removing the starter. Unplug the starter and stow it away from flammable objects. Do not return it to storage until it has cooled completely.

Non-Toxic, Paraffin and Sawdust Starters: These cubes, sticks or blocks can aid in lighting charcoal and can also be used with a chimney starter instead of newspaper. Paraffin starters look like wax ice cubes. Sawdust starters are similar to pressed logs used in fireplaces, but come in sticks that are about 5 inches long.

Lighting a Gas Grill

First, open the lid. Failure to do this before lighting could allow a dangerous buildup of gas. Make sure all the burner knobs are turned to off, then turn on the gas at the source. Read the owner's manual and follow instructions for lighting the burners. If your grill has an automatic ignition, you probably need to turn on one particular burner before you press the ignition switch. You should be able to hear the whoosh of the gas lighting.

If the automatic ignition does not work, you can usually light the grill manually through an ignition hole located in the front or side of the grill. If the grill is still not on after 1 minute, shut off the burner and wait a few minutes for the gas to dissipate before trying again. Gas grills generally need to preheat for 10 to 15 minutes with the burners on high and the cover closed before cooking begins.

Why won't my gas grill light?

1. You forgot to turn on the gas at the tank.

2. You forgot to turn on the gas burner or turned on the wrong one.

3. Hoses are clogged or bent. Dirt or insect debris are blocking the venturis (the metal conduits that carry gas to the burners).

4. The automatic ignition system is not sparking. Try lighting the grill manually according to your owner's manual.

5. You're out of gas!

Fuel for Thought

Before you light your fire you must choose your fuel, of course. This used to be a simple matter of picking up a bag of charcoal. It still can be, but we now have choices.

Charcoal Briquets: The original briquets were produced in the 1920's as a by-product of Henry Ford's automobile plants. Scrap wood was mixed with binders to produce a convenient, uniform product. There are differences in what goes into briquets depending on the brand, although contrary to urban myth, most do not contain petroleum products. You can also purchase pure wood briquets in many natural food stores.

Lump Charcoal: These irregular shaped hunks of charred wood are made without binders or fillers. They burn faster, hotter and less regularly than briquets. They are also more expensive.

Hardwood Chunks: Oak, mesquite, hickory and fruit woods make a fragrant natural fuel for grilling. They burn even faster than lump charcoal and are also pricey. More often chunks of these woods are soaked and used to create smoke that flavors food. Never use soft wood, such as pine or fir, since it produces a potentially dangerous (and not very tasty) sooty residue. Never use lumber, plywood or any wood that has been chemically treated. Most home centers and hardware stores carry hardwood chunks for grilling and smoking.

Hardwood Types for Smoking

Hickory: a pungent, classic barbecue smoke flavor

Mesquite: a bold, slightly sweeter smoke flavor

Cherry: a fruity, slightly sweet smoke flavor

Alder: a delicate smoke flavor for fish or lighter meats

Taming the Flames

Anyone who has been served grilled chicken that's burnt black outside, but still raw inside knows that there's more to grilling than building a fire. You need to control the heat and understand the cooking process that's right for the food you want to grill.

In general, thin pieces of meat, fish or vegetables can go over a direct fire at a high temperature for a short time. By the time the outside has grill marks, the interior is cooked through. This method doesn't work for big hunks of meat or for tougher cuts like pork ribs that need long slow heat to become tender. That's why you need to understand direct and indirect grilling.

Direct Versus Indirect Grilling

There's probably more confusion about these two expressions than any other part of the grilling vocabulary. In the simplest terms, direct grilling is cooking over the heat source. Indirect means what it sounds like it: cooking in heat, but not right over a fire. Direct grilling is perfect for burgers, brats, steaks and kebabs. Indirect grilling is for food that takes more than

30 minutes to cook, such as a whole chicken, pork shoulder or leg of lamb. It's always done in a covered grill.

Direct Grilling over Charcoal

To make a direct fire for charcoal grilling, spread the lit coals around with a long-handled implement—tongs, spatula or even a garden hoe work well. You want an even layer of coals, but you may want to leave an area to one side free of charcoal. This will give you a place to move food that is cooking too quickly or that is causing a flare-up. You can take this notion even further by creating a direct fire that will provide three different cooking temperatures. Pile a double layer of lit charcoal on one side of the fire box, a single layer in the middle and leave one side fire-free. You'll have hot heat for searing, medium high for direct grilling and a safety zone.

Direct Grilling on a Gas Grill

Nothing could be easier. Remember to preheat the grill for 10 or 15 minutes on high

before you start cooking. You can leave one burner off to give yourself a fire-free zone for rescuing food that is cooking too fast or causing flare-ups.

Indirect Grilling over Charcoal

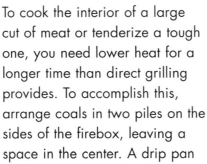

To cook the interior of a large cut of meat or tenderize a tough one, you need lower heat for a longer time than direct grilling provides. To accomplish this, arrange coals in two piles on the sides of the firebox, leaving a space in the center. A drip pan (a disposable aluminum pan) is placed in the center space to collect the fat. The food goes on the grid over the drip pan.

In order to keep the fire going, you'll need to replenish the coals at regular intervals. A hinged cooking grid is very helpful since you'll need to add 8 to 10 coals to each side of the fire as needed—at least every hour with a fire from briquets, or every 25 to 30 minutes if you're burning lump charcoal.

If you add briquets directly to the existing fire, leave the cover off the grill until they catch. You can also start additional coals in a chimney starter. (Make sure it's on concrete or other nonflammable surface.)

Indirect Grilling over Gas

Preheat all burners on high as usual. Then turn off the burner that will be directly under the food. Adjust the other burners to the temperature suggested in the recipe. A drip pan is not always necessary since many gas grills have built in catch pans. You may need a drip pan for a fatty food, like duck, however. Some manufacturers recommend grilling some foods on a rack placed in an aluminum pan on the cooking grid. Consult your owner's manual for the best results.

Clock Watcher

Starting charcoal in a chimney:	15 to 25 minutes
Preheating a gas grill:	10 to 15 minutes
Charcoal briquet fire lasts:	50 to 60 minutes
Lump charcoal fire lasts:	25 to 30 minutes
Time to grill a ¾-inch burger:	10 to 20 minutes
Time to grill a 2-inch steak:	20 to 24 minutes
Time to grill a 15 pound turkey:	4½ hours

NOTE: All times will vary depending on the size of the grill, kind of fuel and weather conditions.

A Handy Way to Judge Heat

Place your hand four inches above the cooking grid. Count how many seconds before the intensity of the heat makes you remove your hand.

High Heat	(400°F+)	1 to 2 seconds
Medium-High Heat	(375°F)	2 to 3 seconds
Medium Heat	(350°F)	4 to 5 seconds
Low	(250°F)	5 to 6 seconds

Flare-Ups and How to Handle Them

The bugaboo of every griller, flare-ups happen when grease drips onto hot coals or burners. Flames licking around your food may be exciting to watch, but a charred, blackened surface definitely does not improve flavor. (It's not healthy eating either. According to the USDA, eating charred food increases exposure to carcinogens.) Almost every serious griller has his or her own favorite way of taking care of a flare-up.

Spray Bottle of Water or Water Pistol: A spray of water will usually quell the flames in a charcoal grill—temporarily. The trouble is, it won't eliminate the grease, so chances are it will flare up again. Of course, if you continue to spray on water, you'll eventually extinguish the fire.

Move the Food: It's much better to move the food to a part of the grid where it's not directly over the fire.

That way the fat can burn off the grid without hurting the food. You can achieve this by leaving a fire-free zone when you build your fire, or by moving food to a warming rack. If necessary, you can even take food off the grill for a few moments until the grease on the grid burns off.

Prevention: If you trim meat of unnecessary fat before grilling and go easy on the oil in the marinade, there's less chance of a flare-up. It also helps to drain off most of the marinade before placing food on the grid. If you're experiencing a lot of flare-ups you should thoroughly clean your grill.

Playing with Fire

It's relaxing to cook outdoors and easy to forget that there are very real risks involved in grilling. According to the U.S. Consumer Product Safety Commission, every year at least 30 people are injured as a result of gas grill fires or explosions, and another 30 die as a result of carbon monoxide fumes from using charcoal indoors. Here are some common-sense precautions to keep you from becoming a statistic.

Before You Grill

• Read and follow the instruction manual that comes with your grill. If you have questions, contact the manufacturer for clarification.

• Place your grill at least 10 feet away from your house or any other building. NEVER use a grill in a garage, breezeway, carport or porch. NEVER place a grill on a flammable surface, like a wooden deck. Most important of all—NEVER use gas or charcoal indoors.

• A grill needs to be on level ground. Try to find a spot with good ventilation that is protected from heavy winds.

Make sure the grill is steady and not tilted.

• Have a dry chemical fire extinguisher on hand and know how to use it. A bucket of sand is handy to have around to dump on a ground fire. Remember that water does not put out a grease fire.

• Dress the part. Don't grill in loose clothing that could catch fire. Tie back your hair if it is long. Shorts and flip-flops may be your summertime uniform, but they won't protect you from flying sparks or dripping grease.

• Have thick oven mitts and potholders available.

• Make sure electrical accessories (for example, rotisserie) are properly grounded.

• On a gas grill, especially one that

hasn't been used in a while, check grill hoses and connectors for cracking, brittleness, holes and leaks. Make sure there are no kinks in any hoses. Check for gas leaks according to the manufacturer's instructions. NEVER use a match to check for a leak. If you think there is a leak or smell gas, do NOT light the grill.

While You Grill

• Keep kids and pets away from the grill and never, ever leave a lit grill unattended. It only takes a millisecond for an accident or burn to happen. At high temperatures every part of a grill is superheated. (Charcoal can reach 1,000°F!) Keep anything flammable, including lighter fluid bottles and extra propane tanks, away from the grilling area.

• Set up ingredients and equipment ahead of time so you can devote your attention to the fire while cooking. Have your ingredients and condiments ready to go. The same goes for the tools you'll need, like long-handled spatulas, tongs, basting brushes and oven mitts. That way you won't be tempted to leave the grill unattended "just to get a salt shaker."

• Don't allow games or other activities near the grill. Remember that the grill stays hot long after the cooking is over, too.

Special Tips for Charcoal Safety

• NEVER burn charcoal inside, not even in a portable grill or hibachi, not even with ventilation. Poisonous carbon monoxide fumes are colorless and odorless and very lethal. The same rules apply to charcoal disposal. Do NOT store a grill indoors that contains freshly used coals.

• NEVER use an electric starter in the rain or when standing on wet ground. After the coals are lit, unplug the starter, remove it from the coals and be careful where you put it. Let it cool completely before storing.

• When using instant-light briquets, don't add lighter fluid. Do not use electric or chimney starters either. Also, do not add instant-light briquets to replenish an existing fire. Use regular charcoal.

• NEVER use kerosene or gasoline to light charcoal. Do NOT add charcoal lighter to an existing fire, even if the fire looks like it is out or is only warm.

• Use a flame-retardant, heavy mitt when handling any part of the grill (even a wooden handle can get hot). Rearrange coals with long handled implements.

• Let coals burn out completely and allow ashes to cool for 48 hours before disposing of them.

Special Tips for Gas Grill Safety

• Propane (also known as LP Gas or Liquid Petroleum) is flammable and the fumes can be explosive. Always read and follow the grill manufacturer's instructions for connecting and removing the propane tank.

• NEVER ask an LP dealer to overfill your tank. The typical cylinder holds about 20 pounds of propane. There must be room for the liquid to expand.

• Always keep propane tanks in a secure upright position. When transporting tanks, do not leave them in a hot car or trunk. Heat can cause the relief valve to open and gas to escape.

• Do NOT store tanks in enclosed spaces, like garages or basements. Keep spare tanks far from your grill or anything else flammable. NEVER store tanks in an area where temperatures might exceed 120°F.

• NEVER connect or remove a propane tank when the grill is in operation or is hot.

• When you're through grilling, turn off the propane at the tank in addition to turning off the burners.

• Keep gas hoses away from hot surfaces and dripping grease. If you can't move the hoses, install a heat shield to protect them.

• Replace gas connectors at the first sign of damage, scratching or nicking—BEFORE they begin leaking. Never use a propane tank that is dented, gouged, corroded or otherwise damaged.

• Do NOT smoke or light matches when inspecting, filling or lighting gas grills or propane tanks.

• If you smell gas or think there is a leak, turn off the tank at the source. Have the tank repaired at an LP gas dealer or by a qualified appliance person. Do not attempt to fix it yourself.

Was it the Potato Salad?
Food Safety and Grilling

The things that make an ideal grilling season—hot weather, lazy afternoons, feasts set out in the shade on a picnic table—are ideal for bacteria, too. A few simple precautions can keep your food safe.

Wash Your Hands Often

Use soap, hot water and suds for about 30 seconds. Wash your hands before handling food, again if you handle raw meat, and once again before serving or eating.

Chill Out

Keep hot foods hot and cold foods cold. This starts at the supermarket. If you're buying perishables on a hot day, it's a good idea to bring along an ice chest to keep things cool in the car. Always refrigerate perishables within 2 hours; make that 1 hour when it's over 90°F.

Don't take meat or poultry out of the refrigerator until you're ready to grill it. If food is stored in a cooler, keep it out of the sun and avoid opening it too often. It's wise to pack drinks in a separate cooler which is likely to be opened a lot.

Don't leave perishable food (including potato salad!) sitting unrefrigerated for longer than 2 hours—1 hour if it's 90°F or more. If you need to hold the burgers or steak, keep them in an oven at 200°F, not sitting out at room temperature.

Separate Raw and Cooked

It's easy to forget this important food safety rule when you're readying food for the grill and making the potato salad at the same time. Virtually all raw meat, poultry and seafood harbor bacteria. This is not ordinarily a problem, since bacteria are destroyed by cooking. It is a serious problem if you forget and start chopping the celery for the salad on the same cutting board or with the same knife you used to prepare the chicken or sausage.

In food-safety language this is called "cross contamination." It is one of the most common causes of food-borne illness. Make sure you keep raw and cooked foods separate at all times. Raw meat, poultry and seafood should never come in contact with food that will be served uncooked (like salad

Food Safety Never-Never Land

1. NEVER put cooked meat or poultry back on the same plate you used to carry it out to the grill.

2. NEVER leave perishable food on a buffet in hot weather for more than 1 hour.

3. NEVER prepare salads or uncooked side dishes using the same cutting board, knife or other utensils that came in contact with raw meat. Always wash your hands after touching raw meat.

4. NEVER use the same brush to baste raw and cooked items on the grill.

5. NEVER serve a marinade used for raw meat or poultry as a sauce unless it has been boiled for at least 1 minute.

fixings) or with food that is already cooked (like prepared vegetables). Don't put the cooked chicken or burgers on the same platter you used to bring them out to the grill when they were raw. Wash counters, hands and equipment that have touched raw meat or poultry before they come in contact with any other food.

Marinate Safely

Many grilling recipes call for marinating meat to boost flavor. Make sure the used marinade doesn't boost bacteria counts, too. The safest

USDA Safe Internal Temperatures for Meat

Ground Beef, Pork, Veal or Lamb	160°F
Ground Poultry	165°F
Poultry Breasts	170°F
Poultry Thighs, Wings and Legs	180°F
Whole Chicken or Turkey*	180°F
Beef, Veal and Lamb (steaks, chops, roasts)*	
Medium Rare	145°F
Medium	160°F
Well Done	170°F
Fresh Pork (chops, roasts, tenderloin)	
Medium	160°F
Well Done	170°F

For roasts and large cuts of meat, take into account the fact that temperatures continue to rise by several degrees after you remove meat from the grill.

practice is to set aside some of the marinade ahead of time. Then you can discard the marinade that was used for the meat, and baste or sauce with the reserved portion.

If you do use a meat marinade for basting, do NOT baste during the last 5 minutes of grill time, and

don't use the same basting brush for raw and cooked items. If you want to serve used marinade as a sauce, you must boil it for at least 1 minute to make it safe.

Grill Meat to a Safe Internal Temperature

If you think you can tell visually that a burger has been cooked to a safe temperature, think again. According to the USDA, one out of every four burgers turns brown in the middle before it has reached a safe internal temperature (and some pink-inside burgers are perfectly safe!). The color of a meat's interior is NOT a reliable way to judge food safety. The only accurate way to know whether meat has been cooked long enough to kill harmful bacteria is to use a meat thermometer or an instant-read thermometer.

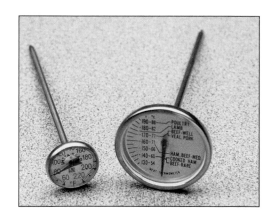

Grilling Tools and Tricks

The number of gadgets, tools and toys available for grillers is mind-boggling. They range from necessary equipment to nice-to-have gadgets to items that are downright silly. (How many folks really need a branding iron to mark steaks rare, medium or well-done?)

Must-Haves

Grill Brush: This is the tool you will use more than once at every grilling session, so don't skimp on the quality. There are many styles of grill brushes but most feature a long wooden handle and a brush made of brass bristles. (Check your owner's manual for specific cleaning instructions for your grill.) They usually also have a scraper at the end to get off the really stubborn stuff. There is also a y-shaped bristle brush available that is designed to fit around individual bars of a grid and get stuck-on food off the side of the bar.

Tongs: These could be the most important grilling tool you own. Invest in long (14 to 16 inches), sturdy tongs. Scalloped ends will give you a firm grip on slippery chicken or vegetables. (The standard tongs you may have in your kitchen with the looped metal ends are pretty much guaranteed to slip on grilled foods.) Choose tongs that are tough enough not to bend if you need to pick up half a chicken or a gargantuan steak. Good-quality tongs are generally spring loaded and many also have a locking feature which makes them easier to store. Restaurant supply stores carry a huge selection of chef-style tongs at very reasonable prices. Some tongs are designed specifically for grilling with wooden handles that stay cool.

Spatula: How else would you turn a burger? Look for long, angled handles, preferably made of stay-cool wood. The blade needs to be a decent size and thin enough to easily slide under a piece of food.

Holes or slits in the blade let grease or juice drip through. There are even special spatulas made with very wide blades to turn large delicate items like fish fillets without breaking them.

Thermometers: It's nice to have a thermometer mounted on your grill to let you know the temperature inside. It's more important to have a thermometer you can use to tell when food is ready to take off the grill. Choose a heatproof meat thermometer you can leave in the food, or an instant-read thermometer, which will give you the internal temperature of any item in a matter of seconds. You can even purchase a barbecue fork with a built-in meat thermometer. For a bit more money, there are thermometers with a probe you leave in the meat while it cooks. A wire runs from the thermometer to an outside read-out that beeps to let you know a specified temperature has been reached.

Barbecue Mitts: Make sure you have heavy-duty, flame-resistant mitts to protect your hands and forearms. For maximum protection, choose mitts or gloves made specially for grilling.

Barbecue Fork: Don't use this to stab the meat and poke holes in it—that will drain precious juices onto the coals! Instead use a barbecue fork to lift large roasts or whole birds when they're done cooking. Barbecue forks are also indispensable for carving.

Basting Brush: Look for a natural bristle brush with a long handle. Nylon bristles will melt if they touch the hot grid. Always wear a barbecue mitt while basting to protect yourself from sudden flare-ups.

Herbal Basting Brush: Make a brush by tying together herb branches. Rosemary works particularly well.

Drip Pans: These simple, disposable aluminum pans are necessities. Use them under food to catch fat and drips while indirect grilling. You can also use them to soak wood chips for smoking or as an impromptu cover for selected food on the grill when you want the rest to cook uncovered.

Heavy-Duty Aluminum Foil:
Aluminum foil can be used for everything from lining a catch pan to making a disposable smoker pouch to providing "handles" for a food item that's heavy or difficult to turn. Buy the big roll.

Nice-to-Have

Grill Scrubber: This tough fiber pad on a handle is used to clean grids and fireboxes. Unlike a grill brush, it is usually intended for use when the grill is cool and you're doing an overall cleaning job.

Grill Topper/Vegetable Grate:
These are perforated metal plates you put on top of the grilling grid to cook small pieces of vegetables or anything else that might fall through the grid onto the coals. Grates are also handy for fragile foods like fish fillets and vegetable burgers. Always spray vegetable grates with nonstick cooking spray and preheat them before adding food. Grill woks and grill skillets are similar products but made with sides

that allow you to toss food and cook on your grill in a similar way to stir-frying indoors.

Hinged Wire Baskets: Similar in principle to a vegetable grate, wire baskets come in a variety of sizes and styles. They allow you not only to cook small or delicate pieces of food, but to

easily turn them over. Fish baskets, which are often fish-shaped, are particularly handy if you plan to grill a lot of seafood. Wire baskets have long handles (sometimes they are detachable for storage) to make flipping food easy.

Smoker Box: Gas grillers who wish to add the flavor of hardwood smoke to grilling may want to invest in one of these. A smoker box is a perforated metal box that holds presoaked wood chips and is placed on the grill grid to add hickory, mesquite or other smoke flavors to food.

Grill Grabber/Grate Lifter: This handy tool allows you to lift a hot grid when you need to add more coals. (You don't need one if your grill grid is hinged or you have a gas grill.)

Skewers: There are dozens of shapes and sizes of skewers to choose from. Here are two of the most practical.

- **Bamboo Skewers:** These come in many lengths, are available at most large markets and are disposable. They are useful not only for kebabs, but also for holding together the rings of an onion or a wedge of radicchio so it won't come apart when you turn it. Bamboo skewers should be soaked for 30 minutes before use so they don't burn up too quickly.

- **Metal Skewers:** The best metal skewers are flat-sided to help keep food from spinning around. Some have decorative touches on the handle end and there are even curved skewers if you are tired of going straight. Two-pronged skewers are made for slippery items like shrimp or onions. They hold food steady and flat, even when it's being flipped.

Rib Racks: Cooking a rack of ribs vertically in a rib rack frees up space on the grill for other food (or more ribs!). It also allows fat to drip off more easily and into a smaller space. You can purchase racks to cook poultry, corn and potatoes, too.

Rotisserie: You can purchase an electric rotisserie attachment for many charcoal and gas grills. The rotisserie slowly turns the meat on a spit over the heat. Browning is even and uniform and the meat bastes itself in its own juices as it turns. If you plan to make the investment, buy a rotisserie designed for the model of grill you own and consider the head room needed—at least an inch of space is required above the chicken or other food that's rotating on the spit.

Things You Can Probably Live Without

Marshmallow Fork: Specially made to grill only marshmallows, this fork shows you when they're cooked through to perfection and pops them off with a special lever.

Grilling Apron or Chef's Hat with Silly Saying: "Kiss the Cook" "King of the Grill" "I'm Not Aging I'm Marinating" If you do wear one, make sure it is made of heavy cotton, not synthetic material which can melt.

Grizzly Spit: It's not really for bear meat, but this oversized, battery-operated spit is designed for grilling big hunks of meat over a campfire.

A Grilling Glossary

ash catcher: This shallow metal receptacle under a charcoal grill is designed to catch ashes from burnt charcoal. Often the bottom grill vents can be used as levers to sweep the ashes into the ash catcher.

automatic ignition: Standard equipment on most gas grills, this button allow you to light the propane burners with a single push.

barbecuing: More arguments have occurred over the definition of barbecuing and its difference from grilling than any other words in the outdoor-cooking lexicon. True barbecuing is a low-heat cooking method that uses a covered smoker or pit. Food, such as brisket or ribs, gets its flavor from wood smoke and is basted with a highly seasoned sauce. Today both terms—barbecuing and grilling—are generally used interchangeably (unless you're in Texas).

baste: To brush food with fat or a flavorful liquid as it cooks. When a basting sauce or marinade contains sugar, like barbecue sauce, limit basting to the last few minutes the food is on the grill, since a sweet marinade is quick to burn.

beer-can chicken: This novelty recipe calls for propping a whole chicken vertically on a half-empty beer-can "rack" to cook over indirect heat.

brazier: This is a pan for holding burning coals—in other words, a simple grill minus the cooking grid.

briquet: A briquet is defined as a compacted, brick-shaped mass. Charcoal briquets, the most common fuel for grilling, are pillow-shaped squares of charcoal dust held together with binders (usually some form of starch) and other ingredients to insure long, steady burning. The marketing of charcoal briquets was begun by Henry Ford as a profitable way to use wood scraps left from his auto manufacturing plant. (See also **charcoal**.)

brochette: The French word for "skewer," this term is sometimes used instead of kabob.

catch pan: This pan (also called a drip pan) is located under the firebox on a gas grill and collects grease and other food drippings. Be sure to empty it regularly.

ceramic briquets: These reusable briquets spread the heat evenly and produce smoke from the meat drippings to flavor food on some gas grills.

charcoal: Charcoal is wood that has been left to smoulder without oxygen until it turns to carbon. It may seem odd to think of making a fire with previously burned wood, but charcoal burns hotter and more slowly than ordinary wood. Charcoal is a very common fuel for cooking and heating in many parts of the world.

charcoal grate: This grate fits into the firebox and holds the burning coals in a charcoal grill.

chimney starter: This hollow metal cylinder is designed to light charcoal without lighter fluid. (See page 12.)

cold smoking: This technique is most often used to produce smoked salmon. The food is located far from the fire, so it smokes without actually cooking. This is not a technique to try at home.

cross contamination: The most common cause of food-borne illness, cross contamination, usually occurs when raw meat or poultry comes into contact with food that will be served without cooking. (See page 21.)

direct grilling: The method in which food is cooked directly over the heat source. (See page 15.)

drip pan: This disposable aluminum pan is used to catch fat drippings while indirect grilling.

ember cooking: Ember cooking is roasting food directly in hot coals. It is sometimes used for yams or potatoes; the burnt exterior is scraped off before eating.

firebox: This is the part of the grill that holds the coals in a charcoal grill or surrounds the gas burners in a gas grill.

flare-ups: Small fires that start when grease drips onto charcoal or other hot surfaces are called flare-ups. They are a particular problem when grilling fatty foods. (See page 17 for suggestions on how to handle them.)

flavorizer bars: V-shaped metal heat plates or bars placed over the gas burners in a grill that function like lava rocks or ceramic briquets.

food-borne illness: This is the correct term for what most people refer to as "food poisoning."

gas (or LP) cylinder: This tank is filled with liquid petroleum and is used to fuel most gas grills.

grid: The cooking surface of a grill is referred to as a grid (also called a cooking grate.)

grill basket/grill topper: This grill accessory sits on top of the grid to prevent small items, such as vegetables, from falling through.

grilling: Strictly speaking, grilling is cooking food over hot coals or a fire at a high temperature. However, the term is also used to refer to most kinds of outdoor cookery, including low-heat cooking in a covered grill. In most places, and in this book, the term grilling is used interchangeably with barbecuing.

grill marks: These appetizing sear marks are made by placing food on a preheated grill grid over high heat.

hardwood chunks: Pieces of hardwood, such as hickory, cherry or mesquite, usually used to create flavorful smoke. Hardwood chunks can also be used as a primary fuel, but they burn very quickly.

hibachi: A traditional style of grill in Japan, the hibachi is a small, portable grill with a thick metal firebox and grids placed over the coals. The grids usually have height adjustments so temperature can be controlled by changing the distance between coals and food.

hinged wire baskets: These metal baskets come in many shapes and sizes and are designed to make it easy to flip delicate foods, such as fish fillets or vegetable burgers, without having them stick to the grid or fall apart.

hobo packs: A packet made of aluminum foil and filled with food for the grill, a hobo pack is useful for cooking combinations of foods that will benefit from a mingling of flavors. It also works well to protect extremely fragile foods, such as thin fish fillets.

hot smoking: This is really another name for traditional barbecuing. Food is cooked slowly over low heat for a long time, often with the addition of hardwood chips to provide smoke flavor.

indirect grilling: In this cooking method, food is placed over a drip pan instead of directly over the heat source. Indirect grilling is used for foods that need longer cooking over lower temperatures. (See page 16.)

instant-read thermometer: An invaluable tool for judging doneness of food. The metal probe gives you the internal temperature in a matter of a few seconds.

kabob (or kebab or shish kebab): Small chunks of meat, poultry, vegetables or fish threaded onto a skewer for grilling.

kettle grill: A bowl-shaped charcoal grill with a cover that was invented in 1952; this style of grill has become an icon of backyard grilling.

lava rocks or stones: These porous rock chunks are used in some gas grills to spread the heat evenly and produce flavorful smoke from meat drippings.

liquid petroleum (LP gas) or propane: This is the most common fuel for gas grills. Canisters of LP gas can be purchased, refilled or exchanged at most hardware and home improvement stores.

lump charcoal or charwood: Natural wood charcoal, without binders or additives is called lump charcoal. It burns hotter and faster than charcoal briquets.

marinate: To marinate is to soak food in a seasoned liquid mixture (a marinade) which usually includes an acid.

mesquite: One of the most popular woods for adding flavor to grilled foods, mesquite comes from a low-growing Southwestern tree. Mesquite flavor is often added to charcoal briquets and barbecue sauces.

mop: A liquid basting solution made with spices and herbs, a mop is used to add flavor and moisture to barbecued foods as they cook. Mop also refers to the tool used to apply the liquid which resembles a floor mop.

propane: (See **liquid petroleum**.)

rotisserie: A rotisserie consists of a spit that is inserted through the food to be cooked and then placed in a motor-driven assembly that rotates the food during cooking, allowing it to baste in its own juices and cook more evenly.

rub: A mixture of herbs, spices and seasonings, a rub is massaged into meat or poultry before grilling.

saté: An Indonesian (and southeast Asian) favorite street food, a saté features marinated meat and vegetables skewered kabob-style and grilled. Satés are often served with a spicy peanut dipping sauce.

sear: Sear means to brown meat or poultry quickly by subjecting it to very high heat. While there is disagreement as to whether searing actually seals in juices, it does create a delicious crusty exterior.

skewer: A long, thin, pointed rod made of metal or wood, a skewer is used to impale food for a kabob or saté. Skewers are also useful for holding together onion rings and other food that tend to fall into pieces.

smoker: A traditional smoker consists of a firebox at one end and a cooking or smoking chamber at the other. It can be horizontal or vertical and sometimes includes a chamber to hold liquid for wet smoking. Big horizontal smokers are also called pits.

smoker box/smoker pouch: This is a container designed to hold flavorful wood chips that have been soaked. The smoker box is perforated to allow smoke from the chips to penetrate food that is being grilled. A disposable smoker pouch can be made of heavy-duty foil.

smoke ring: This style of charcoal fire keeps the lit coals in a ring around the outside edge of the grill. The flame-free circle inside is used for indirect grilling or for holding food that is cooking too quickly or charring.

teriyaki: This Japanese marinade is made of soy sauce, ginger, sugar and other seasonings and is frequently used on grilled foods.

two- or three-level fire: A two-level fire is a charcoal fire built with zones of heat created by piling coals in a double layer for high heat and a single layer for medium heat. In a three-level fire there is also an area left entirely free of coals to provide a space to hold food that is charring or cooking too quickly.

vents: These adjustable openings at the bottom and in the cover of a charcoal grill allow oxygen levels to be controlled which modulates the level of heat inside a grill.

wood chips/pellets: Wood chips and pellets come in a variety of flavors, including hickory, mesquite and cherry. After soaking for 1 hour they are added to coals or placed in a smoker box on a gas grill to contribute a smoky flavor to grilled foods. You can also purchase presoaked chips in a box or can that are ready to use.

Here's the Beef—
Burgers, Steaks, Roasts and Ribs

Does it get any better than a steak or burger, seared to crusty perfection outside and dripping with beefy juices inside? Beef and grills were made for each other. Knowing which cuts to grill and how to grill them will help you coax maximum flavor from the meat.

Steps to Burger Perfection

A classic grilled burger is a backyard icon with good reason—it's totally delicious and utterly satisfying. In fact, if you make great burgers, you may have trouble convincing friends and family to let you cook anything else on the grill.

1. Start out with high quality, freshly ground meat.

For the tastiest burger, skip the pre-formed frozen patties and make your own. Most cooks agree that a bit of fat is needed to add flavor—ground chuck with about 15% fat is a good choice. If you're worried about the fat content, take solace in the fact that cooking over coals lets fat drip off creating flavorful smoke.

2. Don't handle the meat too much.

If you knead and squish a lot, the meat will compact and won't be as juicy when it's cooked. Form the patties gently, but firmly. Refrigerating them before grilling helps keep them firm.

3. Don't make the patties too thick.

¾ to 1 inch thick is ideal. Food safety requires that the interior of a burger reach a temperature of 160°F. A really thick burger is likely to be burned outside before it reaches that temperature inside.

4. Preheat the grill.

It's also important to oil the grill after it's preheated. Burgers should sizzle when they hit the grid. High heat keeps them from sticking and gives burgers great grill marks.

5. Don't try to flip too soon.

Let the burgers grill for 3 or 4 minutes. They will release from the grid and be easier to turn. Struggling to flip sooner can break burgers apart.

6. Don't squash the patties!

You'll lose precious juices and flavor if you flatten the burgers with your spatula.

7. Use a thermometer.

Insert an instant-read thermometer into the side of the burger to judge doneness. It should read 160°F. (Remember to remove an instant-read thermometer after using it or it will melt.) The color of the meat's interior is not a reliable way to judge food safety. (See page 22.)

8. Serve them hot with all the fixings.

Set up condiments ahead of time so you won't have to leave the burgers cooling on a platter while you search for ketchup or slice the tomatoes.

How to Grill a Great Steak

Not every steak should be grilled the same way, and understanding the different cuts is the first step to great grilling. The names you see in the butcher case can be confusing. For instance, a strip steak is sometimes called New York strip or shell steak, depending on what part of the country you live in (or where your butcher is from!). Each kind of steak has its fans. In general, tougher, more fibrous cuts, such as skirt steak, offer a bigger beefier flavor. Pricier cuts like filet mignon, are lean and much more tender, but often have a subtler flavor.

Some rules apply to grilling any steak. Trim off all but about ¼ inch of visible fat to prevent flare-ups. Pat steaks dry

to help them brown quickly. Make sure coals have reached high heat or a gas grill is preheated so the meat will sear when it hits the grid. To turn meat, use tongs. Pierce with a fork and you'll lose flavorful juices. Last, but not least, don't overcook!

Ribeye Steak

(also called Delmonico, or when the bone is attached, rib steak): Cut from the small end of the rib roast, ribeye is tender and juicy. In fact, it just may be the perfect steak for grilling. Give it a good sear and cook to the desired degree of doneness. It's hard to go wrong with a ribeye.

Porterhouse and T-Bone Steaks:

These two bone-in cuts feature a strip sirloin portion as well as a piece of the tenderloin (filet mignon) on the smaller side. A porterhouse is generally a larger, thicker steak, cut from the large end of the loin. T-bones come from closer to the center of the animal, so they are slightly more tender, but the tenderloin portion is smaller, too. Both porterhouse and T-bone are great seared over direct heat, then finished over high or medium. If you're cooking a thick porterhouse, be prepared to quickly move it to a cooler section of the grill or turn down the heat if it begins to scorch.

Beyond-the-Basics Burger Toppings

- Grilled mushrooms and onions
- Guacamole or slices of avocado
- Salsa
- Coleslaw
- Herb butter
- Designer mayonnaise (chipotle-, wasabi- or pesto-flavored)
- Grilled peppers
- Corn relish
- Teriyaki sauce
- Pepperoni and mozzarella
- Feta cheese and chopped olives
- Chili
- Giardiniera

Strip Steak (also called New York strip, Kansas City strip, top loin, shell, ambassador, hotel cut, sirloin club): This steak is the top loin minus the tenderloin (the smaller side of a porterhouse or T-bone). Many steak lovers believe the firm texture and meaty flavor of a strip steak are unsurpassed. Purchase a strip steak that's at least ¾ inch thick, sear it and finish over direct high or medium heat.

Getting Good Grill Marks

Those beautiful criss-cross grill marks you see in a fancy steak house are easy to accomplish in your own backyard. Grill marks don't make steak taste any better, but they do make you look like a pro. Here's the secret to making steak look as good as it tastes.

1. Make sure the grid is hot and the meat is dry.

2. Sear the steak over direct heat for 1 or 2 minutes.

3. Lift the steak with a spatula or tongs and rotate it 90°. Don't flip it yet. Cook for another 1 or 2 minutes.

4. Now flip the steak with tongs or spatula. You'll see the criss-cross marks you made on the finished side. Sear the meat another one or two minutes.

5. Turn the steak 90° again without flipping it; continue to cook to the desired degree of doneness.

Filet Mignon (also called tenderloin): A round, relatively small steak, filet mignon is lean and extremely tender. Grill a filet over high heat and be careful not to overcook it.

Sirloin Steak: Sirloin delivers plenty of rich, beefy flavor for a reasonable price. Top sirloin is generally more tender (and expensive) than bottom sirloin. Since it can be tough, sirloin is often marinated and sliced thinly across the grain.

London Broil: Usually a thick cut from the top round or sirloin. (Sometimes flank steak is also called London broil.) This relatively lean cut takes well to marinade and is best grilled to medium doneness and cut into thin slices against the grain.

Flank Steak: This lean, highly flavorful cut can be tough and stringy. It is often marinated and should be cooked to no more than medium doneness. Slice flank steak into thin pieces across the grain to serve.

Skirt Steak: This long, thin cut has always been a Latin American favorite and is the traditional cut for fajitas. Like flank steak, it is lean and full of flavor. Grill skirt steak over high heat to medium-rare and cut across the grain into thin slices.

Beef Roasts and Ribs

As with steaks, knowing the cut of beef you're dealing with is a large part of the battle. Consult the recipe to determine what to buy and the best cooking method. Roasts need to be cooked over indirect heat. (See page 16.) Some roasts—standing rib roast, whole tenderloin—are naturally tender. Others—brisket, tri-tip, chuck—need extra steps (marinating or sealing in foil) to make them tender. Long, slow smoking is often recommended for brisket.

Beef ribs make it to American grills a lot less often than pork ribs. It is a pity because properly cooked (long and slow), beef ribs are seriously delicious. There are two different kinds of beef ribs to choose from.

Beef Short Ribs (also called flanken, chuck short ribs): These are fairly rectangular (about 2 inches by 3 inches) ribs cut from beef chuck so they need long, slow cooking to make them tender. Cross-cut beef ribs are often labeled flanken and are cut across the bone instead of between bones.

Beef Ribs (also called Texas ribs or beef back ribs) look like they came from a mastadon. A full rack (7 ribs) of these giant-sized ribs will feed two. Like short ribs and pork ribs, beef ribs need to be cooked over indirect heat slowly over a long period of time.

BEEF – Time and Temperature Chart

CUT	APPROXIMATE COOKING TIME	INTERIOR TEMP.
Burgers	5 to 6 minutes per side	160°F
Steaks (1 inch thick)	3 to 4 minutes per side for rare	140°F
	4 to 6 minutes per side for medium	160°F
	6 to 7 minutes per side for well-done	170°F
Tenderloin Roast (4 to 5 pounds)	1¼ hours (indirect) for medium	160°F
Beef Ribs	2 hours (indirect)	170°F

High on the Hog

Rib Tips

- One slab of spareribs will serve two to four people. A slab of baby back ribs is one or two servings.

- To cook multiple slabs of ribs at once, invest in a rib rack.

- Add smoky flavor to your ribs by soaking wood chips and adding them to the fire or a smoker box.

- If you don't have the time to make your own barbecue sauce, dress up the store-bought kind by adding some hot sauce, liquid smoke, fresh garlic or ginger, whatever you like.

- To tell when ribs are done, look for a bit of bone protruding from the meat (about 1/4 inch) and see if the meat is tender enough to tear apart with your fingers.

- To keep portions easier to handle, cut cooked racks into one- or two-rib servings.

It's often said that one can eat every part of a pig but the squeal. Just about any part of the pig does well on the grill, too, if you know how to cook it. Proper grilling allows fat to melt away and delicious smoke flavor to penetrate the sweet meat. Pork is so easy to grill and so delectable, usually the main problem is not making a pig of yourself.

Bone Up on Ribs

Buy the right ribs. Look for slabs of ribs with good meat coverage over the bones and no large surface areas of fat. Many fresh pork products sold today have been "enhanced" with a solution of water, salt and flavorings to make them juicier. Check labels and if you do purchase an enhanced product, be aware that you may not need to use as much salt as you would with ordinary ribs.

1. Trim the meat if necessary.

Racks of spareribs are sold either whole or St. Louis style. Whole ribs have a flap of meat on the inside of the ribs; cut this off and grill it alongside the rack. There is also a strip of meat and cartilage along the edge of the slab (rib tips) which should be removed and grilled separately. St. Louis-style ribs have already had these extras removed.

Unless it's been removed by a butcher, all pork ribs have a tough membrane on the interior bony side. Insert a sharp knife tip under the membrane next to a bone; wiggle it around to loosen it. Grab the membrane, using a paper towel to improve your grip, and pull the membrane from the rib rack.

2. Rub them the right way.

It's not absolutely necessary to use a spice rub, but if you don't, be sure to season the ribs with salt and pepper.

3. Cook them slowly.

Pork ribs require indirect heat to cook to fall-off-the-bone tenderness. (See page 16.) It usually takes at least 1½ hours to grill a rack, so prepare accordingly. If you're charcoal grilling, you'll definitely need to add coals along the way.

4. Be savvy about sauce.

Sugar burns very quickly, so any sauce that contains it (This includes virtually every prepared sauce.) should only be brushed on during the last 15 minutes of grilling. Mops, which are traditionally used in southern barbecue, are vinegar based and can be used any time. Keep in mind that there are plenty of options other than traditional tomato-based barbecue sauce.

Types and Styles of Ribs

Baby Back Ribs (also called back ribs, loin back ribs): These ribs are smaller and less fatty than spareribs. They're also more expensive.

Spareribs: These ribs are bigger and longer than baby backs. They need to be cooked slowly for a long time because they can be

tougher, but many rib aficionados claim spareribs are also more flavorful.

St. Louis Spareribs: These are spareribs that have been trimmed of the strip of meat and cartilage along the edge of the slab.

Country-Style Spareribs: These ribs are actually individual pork chops cut from the shoulder area; the bone is part of the shoulder blade. Country-style ribs are big and meaty, but a bit hard to eat because of the bone and fat running though the meat.

Chops, Roasts and More

Pork takes well to many seasonings and is a favorite of grillers from Mexico to Vietnam. (Check the index for recipes for Cuban Garlic and Lime Pork Chops, Javanese Pork Saté and other international ideas.)

The pork that is marketed today is much leaner than it used to be. (A boneless center-cut loin chop has less fat than a boneless, skinless chicken breast!) The good news is that it's low in fat; the bad news is that lean meat dries out and becomes tough very quickly. Fortunately, pork takes to marinades and brines which can add moisture. The real secret is to not overcook—an internal temperature of 160°F is safe and some cuts, like pork tenderloin may still be slightly pink inside.

Pork Chops (loin or rib): Thick or thin, bone-in or butterflied, pork chops cook quickly over direct heat. Chops that are ¾ inch thick cook in only 8 to 10 minutes, so don't wander off and leave them unattended.

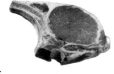

Pork Loin and Pork Tenderloin Roasts: Either of these pork cuts is great for kabobs or satés. Whole larger roasts need to be cooked over indirect heat. (See page 16.) Pork tenderloins are small and thin

(See page 16.)

What is Jerk Anyway?

The simple answer is that jerk is Jamaican barbecue, but jerk is much more. It's a seasoning blend, a sauce, a marinade, a cooking method and in Jamaica, a way of life. There are many versions of jerk seasoning, but most of them include chili peppers, thyme, allspice, garlic and onion.

enough to cook over direct heat. They benefit from a marinade and are so lean they can be overcooked in a heartbeat. It's best to pull a tenderloin off the grill when it reaches an internal temperature of 155°F and let it rest for a few minutes; the temperature will rise to 160°F.

Beware Exploding Sausages!

If a sausage is heated too rapidly steam can build up inside the casing. Steam will cause the casing to split, or worse, to explode like an overinflated meat-filled balloon (not a pretty sight). The solution is to provide a release valve by pricking the sausage before cooking. Don't make the holes too big or too much juice will leak out.

Hot Dog! Sausage on the Grill

It's summertime and the cooking is easy—just throw some dogs or brats on the grill. Even if you've never owned a grill, you've probably cooked a hot dog over a fire at some time in your life so you know the transformation that takes place. Sausages (even hot dogs) become almost a gourmet meal when grilled. There are probably as many varieties of sausage as there are sausage lovers, but they all fall into one of two categories.

Cooked Sausages: Hot dogs are the best known in this category, but it also includes most smoked sausages. Bratwurst come both precooked and raw as do many other varieties, so check the package. These precooked sausages are real no-brainers on the grill—just heat them through and they're good to go.

Raw or Fresh Sausages: Old-fashioned bratwurst, Italian sausage and kielbasa (Polish) sausage are often sold uncooked. These sausages require special handling for food safety reasons. They should be kept separate from cooked food and need to be cooked all the way through (160°F). While this can be done on the grill, it's easy to burn the outside before the inside is cooked. The easier way to accomplish this is to poach or braise sausage first in beer or another flavorful liquid, then brown them on the grill.

PORK – Time and Temperature Chart

CUT	APPROXIMATE COOKING TIME	INTERIOR TEMP.
Ribs	1½ to 2 hours	170°F
Chops/Steaks	4 to 6 minutes per side for medium	160°F
	6 to 8 minutes per side for well done	170°F
Pork Tenderloin Roast (1½ pounds)	12 to 16 minutes for medium	160°F
Sausages	16-20 minutes	160°-170°

Luscious, Luxurious Lamb

Lamb is a favorite meat for grilling around much of the globe. No wonder—the rich, full flavor of lamb benefits from a kiss of smoke and fire like no other. Grilling mellows and softens the flavor of lamb so that even folks who think they don't like it become converts after the first taste. Grilling lamb is amazingly easy, too, since its higher fat content keeps it moist and juicy.

Ground Lamb: A lamb burger is rich, juicy and flavorful. Like other ground meat, ground lamb must be cooked to an internal temperature of 160°F for food safety reasons.

Lamb Chops: Loin or rib chops grill to perfection over direct heat in a matter of minutes. Just be sure to trim excess fat before grilling to avoid flare-ups.

Boneless Lamb Chunks: You can purchase lamb precut for kabobs or cut your own from a lamb leg or steak.

Leg of Lamb: Do you think preparing a leg of lamb on the grill is tricky? You're in for a pleasant surprise, because grilling a butterflied, boneless leg of lamb is quite simple and takes only about 30 minutes. (Check the index for an easy recipe for Rosemary-Crusted Leg of Lamb.) A whole, bone-in leg of lamb is delicious grilled, too, but it takes quite a bit longer since it must be cooked over indirect heat. (See page 16.) Leg of lamb is often sold in two pieces—the sirloin or center-cut portion and the shank portion (the part with the bone sticking out.)

LAMB – Time and Temperature Chart

CUT	APPROXIMATE COOKING TIME	INTERIOR TEMP.
Lamb Burgers	10-15 minutes	160°F
Chops (1 inch thick)	2 to 4 minutes per side for rare	140°F
	4 to 6 minutes per side for medium	160°F
	6 to 8 minutes per side for well-done	170°F
Boneless Butterflied Leg	30 to 45 minutes	160°F
Bone-In Leg (6 to 8 pounds)	2 to 2½ hours (indirect)	160°F

Poultry Perfection

What could be more appealing than the crisp skin and juicy interior of perfectly grilled chicken or turkey? Why does it seem so hard to achieve? Everyone has experienced the dry-as-dust grilled chicken breast or, even worse, the chicken leg that's still raw near the bone. Here's some advice on avoiding the pitfalls and getting the best out of any bird.

1. Overcooking/Undercooking.
It's wise to be very conscious of food safety when you're working with poultry and important to make sure it's cooked through to a safe internal temperature of 180°F (170°F for the breast meat). Invest in an instant-read thermometer and stop when you get to a safe temperature. "Another couple of minutes" can turn perfection into shoe leather.

2. Overhandling.
It's not necessary to turn chicken pieces more than once. The more you open the grill lid, the more you lower the temperature and increase cooking time. Poking chicken pieces with a fork will let juices leak out; instead, turn them with tongs.

3. Cooking Time.
White meat cooks faster than dark and different size pieces take different amounts of time. You need to watch closely and pull pieces as they are done.

4. Food Safety.
Poultry can carry salmonella among other things, so pay attention to safety rules. Wash your hands and all cutting boards, knives and other equipment that comes in contact with raw poultry. Never use the plate or tray you used to carry raw poultry to the grill to transport cooked poultry. (Check pages 21 to 22 for additional cautions.)

5. Flare-Ups.
The fatty skin on poultry can easily cause flare-ups. (Of course, it also keeps the bird moist, so it's better to grill with the skin on and remove it after cooking if you're watching fat calories.) Just trim any excess fat before grilling and move the food to a low-heat zone, if necessary. Make sure you lubricate the grid after it's preheated so poultry skin doesn't stick; drain excess marinade before placing the chicken on the grill.

Every kind of bird (and, in fact, each individual bird) is a little different. Virtually all poultry benefits from a marinade, but any marinade that's been in contact with the raw bird must be discarded before grilling. For the most part, poultry should be cooked over medium or medium-high heat since it's prone to drying out. Carefully read the individual recipe you're

preparing, since many variables influence cooking temperatures and times.

Boneless Skinless Chicken Breasts: These low-fat favorites are quick and delicious on the grill, but boneless, skinless chicken breasts will overcook in a matter of seconds. Unfortunately, it's almost impossible to use an instant-read thermometer on such a thin piece of meat. The solution is not to overcook, but to pull one piece and cut it open to check doneness. It only takes 12 to 15 minutes total to cook a medium-size breast.

Bone-In Chicken Parts: These can be a challenge since dark meat takes longer to cook through than light meat. Be prepared to move the chicken pieces if a flare-up occurs. (This is particularly likely when you're grilling with the skin side down.) Don't try to grill over high heat or the chicken will have charred skin and a raw interior. Instead, to crisp the skin, finish the chicken with the skin side down over high heat for the last 5 minutes of grilling.

Whole or Half Chicken: Indirect medium heat and a drip pan are what you need to grill a whole chicken. (See page 16.) It will take an hour or more, but this one is worth waiting for—succulent and flavorful. A half chicken is just as delicious and cooks faster. Try adding a seasoning paste under the skin for an even tastier treat. Use a thermometer to determine doneness and make sure it is not touching the bone.

Ground Chicken or Turkey: Poultry burgers cry out for zesty seasoning. Try them with Asian or Mexican flavorings.

Whole Turkey: Once you experience a grilled turkey, Thanksgiving will never be the same. Make sure that the bird you buy is small enough to fit comfortably under the lid of your grill with at least an inch

The Brick Trick

Wrap a relatively clean brick in heavy-duty foil and use it as a grilling weight. Placed on top of a split chicken or butterflied game hen, the weight of the brick presses it down to cook evenly and helps create good grill marks, too.

to spare. For food safety reasons, you should not grill a turkey that weighs more than 16 pounds. (It takes bigger birds too long to reach an internal temperature that will destroy harmful bacteria.) For food safety reasons, it's best not to stuff a grill-roasted turkey.

Once the indirect fire is set up, grilling is fairly carefree and the oven is free for other things. (See page 16.) You'll need enough gas or charcoal to keep your grill at a steady, medium, indirect heat for 3½ hours or more depending on the turkey's size.

Turkey Breast or Turkey Tenderloin Roast: These smaller cuts are an excellent way to enjoy a turkey dinner without making it a big deal. Roasts can be purchased bone-in or rolled, whole or half. The tenderloin portion is a thin, tender piece of breast meat perfect for making turkey kabobs or grilling and slicing for sandwiches.

Cornish Game Hens: These miniature chickens weigh in at less than 2½ pounds each. They can be cooked in the same ways as chicken, but are particularly nice butterflied and grilled flat. See the index for a recipe for Butterflied Cornish Game Hens.

POULTRY – Time and Temperature Chart

CUT	APPROXIMATE COOKING TIME	INTERIOR TEMP.
Chicken		
Boneless Breast	4 to 6 minutes per side	170°F
Bone-in Breast	10 to 15 minutes per side	170°F
Legs/Thighs	10 to 15 minutes per side	180°F
Drumsticks	8 to 12 minutes per side	180°F
Wings	8 to 12 minutes per side	until no longer pink near bone
Whole Chicken	15 to 20 minutes per pound (indirect heat)	180°F (measured at thigh)
Turkey		
Turkey Burger (½ inch thick)	4 to 6 minutes per side	165°F
½ Bone-In Breast (2 pounds)	1 to 1½ hours (indirect heat)	170°F
Whole Turkey (unstuffed)	20 to 25 minutes per pound	180°F (measured at thigh)

Seafood Savvy

Do you feel out of your depth when it comes to grilling seafood? Perfectly accomplished grillers who turn out steaks, chops and chicken without thinking twice, often turn to jellyfish when faced with a sea creature. (Cue the theme from "Jaws.") The truth is that grilling most seafood is easy. The fear factor probably comes from the two incontrovertible facts that seafood is both delicate and expensive. It is also perfectly delicious, so put aside any uneasiness, learn a few simple tricks and dive right in.

1. Choose the right variety of fish and the right piece of fish.

Virtually any fish can be grilled, but some varieties, such as sole or flounder, cook so quickly and are so delicate they just aren't a good choice. The other consideration is the cut—a steak versus a fillet. A fish steak is a cross-cut section, often including a piece of the backbone. It is the most forgiving on the grill since it's thick and compact—less likely to fall apart than a fillet. Of course, many delectable kinds of fish aren't available in steak form since they're too small to be cut this way. Fillets do have the advantage of usually being less bony and somewhat easier to eat. If you are grilling fillets, it is helpful to use a fish basket or grill topper.

2. Don't try to turn fish too soon.

As long as you place the fish on a preheated, oiled (and clean!) grid, the time to turn it is when it releases naturally. This generally takes from 5 to 7 minutes. Ease your spatula under a corner of the fish and try lifting. If the fish is sticking, wait a minute and try again.

3. Don't cook fish too long.

This is the biggest fish-grilling sin of all. See the sidebar for instructions on determining doneness. A general rule of thumb is that the cooking time for any fish is about 10 minutes per inch of thickness (measured at the thickest part of the fish.) If you wait until the fish flakes easily as some books instruct, you will have overcooked fish and it will be difficult to remove it from the grid in one piece.

4. Cheat if you need to.

If the fish skin sticks to the grid or your fillet ends up in a

The First and Last Rule for Grilling Seafood: DON'T OVERCOOK

So how do you tell when the fish is done? Peek. Take a knife and gently part the flesh at the thickest part just enough to see inside. The flesh should be just opaque all the way through. (If you grill until the fish "flakes easily" you'll end up with dried out fish.)

dozen pieces, don't despair. Serve some salsa, sauce or chutney on top and nobody will be the wiser. You can also grill fish in foil packets, which eliminates sticking problems entirely. The packet method steams fish to produce a different but still delectable flavor.

Salmon: Steak or fillet, salmon is America's favorite fish with good reason. The rich, full flavor is perfect enhanced with a touch of smoke from the grill. Salmon's bold flavor stands up to strong seasonings—spicy, smoky or sweet.

Tuna: Like salmon, tuna is a fairly fatty fish (the healthful omega-3 kind of fat), so it does well on the grill. It is only available as a steak. Tuna is often served seared on the outside and rare on the inside, because it becomes tough and flavorless if cooked too long. If you prefer your fish cooked through, grill a thinner (½ inch) steak.

Swordfish: A great grilling choice, swordfish is usually sold in the form of a steak. The mild, firm flesh takes well to marinades and is excellent matched with a salsa or chutney. Swordfish is also firm enough to skewer for kabobs.

Halibut: Halibut is a firm, white fish usually marketed as fillets. It's a good grilling fish, but leaner and more delicate than swordfish or salmon.

Mahimahi, Snapper and Seabass: These firm, white fish are sold as fillets or steaks and can be substituted for each other in most recipes. All of these fish are mild in flavor and benefit from a short marinade and zesty seasoning.

Catfish and Trout: These fish are often farm raised, so they're very affordable. The fillets can fall apart fairly easily when you try to turn them, but they are usually thin enough to cook through without flipping. Believe it or not, small whole catfish or trout are easier to handle. One whole fish will make one or two servings. Stuff the cavity with lemon slices or fresh herbs and use a fish basket for easy grilling.

Shellfish—Shrimp, Lobster and Scallops: The same number one rule applies to cooking shellfish as to fish—don't overcook it. Shrimp are done when the shells turn uniformly pink. Lobster and scallops should be cooked only until opaque in the center. Be especially careful with scallops which cook quickly and become rubbery in a matter of seconds.

Beginner's Fishing Lesson

1. Start with an easy-to-grill fish steak (not a fillet) like swordfish or tuna.

2. Use a grill topper or fish basket to minimize sticking.

3. Grill on a clean grid.

4. Oil the grid (or grill topper or basket) as well as the fish right before cooking.

5. Don't try to turn the fish too soon. It will release naturally when it's time to flip.

Vegetables on the Fire

Why limit the great flavor smoke adds to food to the main course? Grilling brings ordinary vegetables to luscious new levels. The direct heat concentrates flavors by cooking out water. Natural plant sugars become caramelized. The results will amaze and delight you—grilling seems to bring out the best in each individual vegetable. Sweet potatoes become sweeter; mushrooms taste meatier. Best of all, you can give up the hassle of leaving the meat sizzling outside, to run back into the kitchen and prepare side dishes. Why bother when everything tastes better from the grill?

So Many Vegetables, So Many Ways to Grill Them

Most vegetables cook quickly and easily over direct medium heat (exceptions are root and other large, dense vegetables). Vegetables need a bit of oil to keep them from sticking to the grid and to maximize flavor. Keep your work easier by cutting pieces to similar sizes. You can also help even out cooking times by cutting slower cooking veggies into thinner pieces or parcooking them first in the microwave. Whatever methods you choose, it won't be hard to convince anyone to eat their vegetables when they're hot off the grill.

Asparagus: Truly delicious from the grill, asparagus is a must-try. Trim tough ends, brush stalks with olive oil and season with salt and pepper. Roll them over with tongs about halfway through the 6 to 8 minutes of cooking time. The only "trick" is to lay the stalks on the grid perpendicular to the bars so they don't fall through.

Bell Peppers: All colors and varieties of peppers can be roasted either whole or cut into pieces. If you wish to peel them, remove the peppers from the grill once the skins are blackened and place them in a closed paper bag or covered dish for about 3 minutes. The charred skin will slip off easily. A medium whole pepper needs about 12 minutes to become charred all around. Slices of pepper will be ready in 6 to 8 minutes, turning once.

Corn: There is plenty of heated discussion about the very best way to grill sweet corn. Fortunately, there is no wrong way to do it.

- **In the husk:** Peel back the husk (but leave it attached) to remove the silk if you like. Soak the corn in its husk in cold water for 30 minutes. Grill for 25 to 30 minutes, rolling the corn with tongs until the husk is charred. Serve in the husk and let diners peel their own ear and leave the husk attached to use as a handle.

- **Husked:** Cook husked ears over direct heat for 10 to 12 minutes, rolling the ears over to get all sides browned. Brush with melted butter while they cook. Add some salt, pepper, lime juice or cayenne pepper to the melted butter for extra zip.

Eggplants: Eggplants come in many shapes, sizes and colors. Cooking methods vary depending on the type of eggplant and how you plan to serve it. Cut regular eggplants crosswise into ½-inch-thick slices and cook about 5 minutes per side. Small, skinny Asian eggplants can be cut in half lengthwise and grill in about 12 minutes. If you wish to make an eggplant dip or puréed eggplant, leave the vegetable whole and grill until the skin is charred (20 to 30 minutes); then peel off the charred skin and mash the flesh.

Garlic: Mellow and buttery, grilled garlic is an awesome accompaniment to anything from a baguette to a pizza. Remove the loose papery skin and cut off the very top of the head to expose the cloves. Drizzle the garlic with a bit of olive oil and wrap it securely in foil. Grill the packet over medium indirect heat 30 to 40 minutes or until soft. (You can stow it on a grill rack or in a cooler corner of the grill while you're cooking everything else.)

Mushrooms: Grilled portobellos make a tasty side dish or excellent vegetarian main course. Oil or marinate them and grill, cap side down, then turn. It will take 12 to 15 minutes total depending on the mushroom's size. Small mushrooms, such as button or brown mushrooms, should be threaded onto skewers for easy handling.

Onions: Sliced onions reveal a sweet new personality when grilled. Cook ½-inch-thick slices about 10 minutes. To keep the rings from slipping apart, skewer them horizontally before grilling.

Potatoes:

- **New Potatoes or Fingerlings:** Toss small potatoes with melted butter or oil and seasonings. If some are larger, cut the bigger ones into halves or quarters first. You can cook them in a grill basket or make a potato kabob. Hobo packs (foil pouches) filled with potatoes and herbs also work very well.

- **Russets, Yukon Gold or Red Potatoes:** To cook large whole potatoes on the grill, try microwaving them first for several minutes. Finishing on the grill will add a smoky flavor in a minimum

amount of time. Potatoes may also be cut into wedges or coins and grilled for 10 to 20 minutes.

Squash (Zucchini or Yellow): Small squash can be halved; larger ones can be cut crosswise or lengthwise into ½-inch-thick slices. Be sure to oil and season them well before grilling for about 8 minutes over direct heat. Chunks of squash also make good kabob ingredients.

Sweet Potatoes: The smoky richness of grilled sweet potatoes is a revelation. To grill sweets whole, microwave first for 2 or 3 minutes and finish on the grill. They're done when they yield to gentle pressure. Squeeze them with your hand protected by a barbecue mitt. Sliced sweet potatoes are also delicious. Simply cut them into ½-inch-thick slices and grill until tender. There's no need to peel them first.

Tomatoes: One taste of a fire-roasted tomato and you'll wonder why you didn't try it sooner. Small or plum tomatoes can be grilled whole, either skewered or in a grill basket. They're ready in about 10 minutes. Larger tomatoes can be halved and grilled with the skin side down. Tomatoes are done when their skins are blistered all over and blackened in spots. Take care when removing them from the grill since they can fall apart—use a spatula, not tongs.

Marinades, Rubs and Sauces

Smoke and fire bring unmatched flavor to grilled food. The wonders worked by seasonings, marinades, rubs and sauces add countless more delights to the griller's repertoire. There are hundreds of brands of prepared barbecue sauces to choose from at supermarkets and specialty stores. (There's even a "Barbecue Sauce of the Month Club.") Plenty of marinades and seasoning rubs designed for grilling are also available. Lots of these ready-made products are excellent. But even if you only use store-bought, it's good to have an understanding of what goes into these flavorings and how to use them.

1. There are two basics you shouldn't grill without.
Salt and pepper are such obvious ingredients that it's easy to underestimate their importance. Certainly you can use the salt and pepper shaker from the table to season food destined for the grill, but there's a better way. Instead of free-flowing, iodized table salt, try kosher salt instead. The larger, flatter crystals cling to food better and there's no off taste from the additives used in regular salt. A pepper mill will give you not only freshly ground pepper, but usually a choice of grinds as well, from coarse to fine. This can make a big flavor difference in a seasoning rub or on a hearty steak. Remember to take note of the salt content of any prepared seasonings or marinades you use and adjust how much salt you add accordingly.

Balsamic Marinade

Makes 1 cup marinade

- 2 pounds beef, pork, lamb or veal
- ½ cup FILIPPO BERIO® Olive Oil
- ½ cup balsamic vinegar
- 2 cloves garlic, slivered
- 1 teaspoon dried oregano leaves
- ½ teaspoon salt
- ½ teaspoon dried marjoram leaves
- ¼ teaspoon freshly ground pepper

Place meat in shallow glass dish. In small bowl, whisk together olive oil, vinegar, garlic, oregano, salt, marjoram and pepper. Pour marinade over meat, using about ½ cup for each pound of meat. Turn to coat both sides. Cover; marinate several hours or overnight, turning meat occasionally. Remove meat; boil marinade 1 minute. Grill meat, brushing frequently with marinade.

Rosemary Garlic Rub

Makes 4 servings

  2 tablespoons chopped fresh rosemary
1½ teaspoons LAWRY'S® Seasoned Salt
  1 teaspoon LAWRY'S® Garlic Pepper
  ½ teaspoon LAWRY'S® Garlic Powder with Parsley
  1 pound beef top sirloin steak
  1 tablespoon olive oil

In small bowl, combine rosemary, Seasoned Salt, Garlic Pepper and Garlic Powder with Parsley; mix well. Brush both sides of steak with oil. Sprinkle with herb mixture, pressing onto steak. Grill or broil steak 15 to 20 minutes or until desired doneness, turning halfway through grilling time.

Meal Idea: Serve with oven roasted or French fried potatoes and honey coated carrots.

Hint: This rub is also great on lamb or pork.

2. A little dip in a marinade can change everything.

It's a marinade that makes saté or tandoori taste authentic. No other method of seasoning is as powerful as a marinade or as easy to use. Most marinades contain an acid ingredient (lemon juice, wine) to tenderize and an oil to add moisture and flavor. In fact, almost any vinaigrette is basically a marinade and can be used as such.

3. Marinate the easy way.

Resealable plastic food storage bags are ideal for marinating. Place the food in the bag, pour the marinade over, squish the air out, seal and refrigerate. Put the bag in a dish to catch any leaks. (If you don't, it's guaranteed to leak!) You can also marinate in a glass or other nonreactive dish. Cover it tightly to keep as much air out as

possible. Never use aluminum, which can discolor and leave a metallic taste in the food. It's a good idea to turn the food once or twice to redistribute the marinade.

4. Marinate safely.

(See page 22 for details.) It's best to discard used marinade, so if you wish to use some for a sauce, reserve it ahead of time. NEVER serve used marinade as a sauce without boiling it for at least 1 minute.

5. Rub things the right way.

A dry rub is nothing more than a blend of spices and herbs. The right one will not only season, it will help to

Mix-and-Match Marinade Chart

Choose one or more ingredients from each category to come up with your signature grilling marinade.

ACID INGREDIENTS
lemon or lime juice
orange juice
vinegar
wine
yogurt

OIL INGREDIENTS
olive oil
canola oil
flavored oils (basil, garlic, etc)
sesame oil
peanut oil

SEASONING INGREDIENTS
brown sugar
chili sauce
fresh ginger
garlic
herbs, fresh or dried
honey
hot sauce
mustard
onions or scallions
soy sauce
spices
Worcestershire sauce

Too Much of a Good Thing

The acid ingredient in a marinade will cause the food to become mushy if it is left soaking too long. How long is too long? It depends on the strength of the marinade and the kind of food. Fish and vegetables should only be marinated briefly—less than 30 minutes. Large pieces of meat can soak overnight. Smaller chops or chicken pieces need from 1 to 4 hours.

Saucy Additions to Store Bought Barbecue Sauce

capers
fresh herbs
ginger
hoisin sauce
horseradish
hot sauce
liquid smoke
mustard
olives
orange marmalade
soy sauce
strong coffee
sun-dried tomatoes

build a flavorful crust on the exterior of meat or poultry. A rub can be as simple as a seasoned salt or as complex as a blend of 20 different spices. Most contain salt, a sweet component, something earthy or herbal and at least a touch of spicy heat.

A wet rub is also called a seasoning paste and contains either oil or another liquid ingredient.

To apply a rub, massage it into the meat or poultry with your fingers, or you can pat or sprinkle it on. If possible, let the meat rest in the refrigerator for 30 minutes to 1 hour.

6. The sauce is the boss.

Americans will argue long and hard over what makes the best barbecue sauce. In Texas it's tomato based and fiery hot. In Kansas City it's sweet and smoky. In North Carolina the favored barbecue sauce for pulled pork is mostly mouth-puckering vinegar. Every sauce seems to have a "secret"

ingredient—coffee, ginger ale, chipotle peppers, beer. Even if you've found a bottled sauce you love, consider adding a special touch to make it your own so that you can have bragging rights. (Part of the fun is refusing to reveal your secret ingredient.)

There's only one trick to using barbecue sauce, and that's to wait until the food is almost done before slathering it with sauce. If you start basting with a sweet sauce too soon, it will burn into an unappetizing sticky charred mess. Wait until the last 10 minutes and set aside a bowl of sauce to serve at the table.

Sweet 'n' Smoky BBQ Sauce

Makes about 1½ cups sauce

- ½ cup ketchup
- ⅓ cup **French's®** Bold n' Spicy Brown Mustard
- ⅓ cup light molasses
- ¼ cup **French's®** Worcestershire Sauce
- ¼ teaspoon liquid smoke or hickory salt (optional)

Combine ketchup, mustard, molasses, Worcestershire and liquid smoke, if desired, in medium bowl. Mix until well blended. Brush on chicken or ribs during last 15 minutes of grilling.

Recipes To Fire Up Your Grilling

You'll find plenty of great ideas to spark your imagination in the pages that follow. There are more than 150 recipes, including new takes on familiar classics like ribs and sausage, as well as exotic detours, such as Cuban Garlic and Lime Pork Chops and Chicken Tikka (Tandoori-Style Grilled Chicken).

Every recipe is easy to follow and makes the most of the incredible flavor you can only get from cooking outdoors. There are so many delectable dishes and mouthwatering photos you'll want to have plenty of charcoal (or gas) on hand before you start browsing. Chances are these pages will be smoke- smudged and sauce-decorated after just one grilling season, and that's just the way it should be.

The Classic Grill

Backyard Barbecue Burgers

1½ pounds ground beef
⅓ cup barbecue sauce, divided
1 to 2 tomatoes, cut into slices
1 onion, cut into slices
1 to 2 tablespoons olive oil
6 kaiser rolls, split
Green or red leaf lettuce

1. Prepare grill for direct grilling. Combine ground beef and 2 tablespoons barbecue sauce in large bowl. Shape into six 1-inch-thick patties.

2. Place patties on grid. Grill, covered, 8 to 10 minutes over medium coals (or, uncovered, 13 to 15 minutes) or until 160°F in centers of patties, turning and brushing often with remaining barbecue sauce.

3. Meanwhile, brush tomato and onion slices* with oil. Place on grid. Grill tomato slices 2 to 3 minutes and onion slices about 10 minutes.

4. Just before serving, place rolls, cut side down, on grid; grill until lightly toasted. Serve patties on rolls with tomatoes, onions and lettuce.   *Makes 6 servings*

Onion slices may be cooked in 2 tablespoons oil in large skillet over medium heat 10 minutes until tender and slightly brown.

Backyard Barbecue Burger

Classic Grilled Chicken

1 whole frying chicken* (3½ pounds), quartered
¼ cup lemon juice
¼ cup olive oil
2 tablespoons soy sauce
2 large cloves garlic, minced
½ teaspoon sugar
½ teaspoon ground cumin
¼ teaspoon black pepper

*Substitute 3½ pounds chicken parts for whole chicken, if desired. Grill legs and thighs about 35 minutes and breast halves about 25 minutes or until chicken is no longer pink in center, turning once.

Rinse chicken under cold running water; pat dry with paper towels. Arrange chicken in 13×9×2-inch glass baking dish. Combine remaining ingredients in small bowl; pour half of mixture over chicken. Cover and refrigerate chicken at least 1 hour or overnight. Cover and reserve remaining mixture in refrigerator to use for basting. Remove chicken from marinade; discard marinade. Arrange medium KINGSFORD® Briquets on each side of large rectangular metal or foil drip pan. Pour hot tap water into drip pan until half full. Place chicken on grid directly above drip pan. Grill chicken, skin side down, on covered grill 25 minutes. Baste with reserved mixture. Turn chicken; cook 20 to 25 minutes or until juices run clear and chicken is no longer pink in center.   *Makes 6 servings*

According to Guinness Book of Records, the biggest attendance at a one-day barbecue was 44,158 people who turned up at Warwick Farm Racecourse, Sydney, Australia on October 10, 1993.

Classic Grilled Chicken

Bodacious Grilled Ribs

4 pounds pork loin back ribs
2 tablespoons paprika
2 teaspoons dried basil leaves
½ teaspoon onion powder
¼ teaspoon garlic powder
¼ teaspoon ground red pepper
¼ teaspoon black pepper
2 sheets (24×18 inches) heavy-duty foil, lightly sprayed with
**   nonstick cooking spray**
8 ice cubes
1 cup barbecue sauce
½ cup apricot all-fruit spread

1. Prepare grill for direct cooking. Cut ribs into 4- to 6-rib pieces.

2. Combine paprika, basil, onion powder, garlic powder, red pepper and black pepper in small bowl. Rub on both sides of rib pieces. Place half of ribs, in single layer, in center of each foil sheet. Place 4 ice cubes on top of each.

3. Double fold sides and ends of foil to seal packets, leaving head space for heat circulation. Place on baking sheet. Stir together barbecue sauce and jam; set aside.

4. Slide packets off baking sheet onto grill grid. Grill, covered, over medium coals 45 to 60 minutes or until tender. Carefully open one end of each packet to allow steam to escape.

5. Open packets and transfer ribs to grill grid. Brush with barbecue sauce mixture. Continue grilling 5 to 10 minutes, brushing with sauce and turning often.

Makes 4 servings

Bodacious Grilled Ribs

Fajitas

2 beef skirt steaks (about 1 pound each)
2 cloves garlic, divided
3 tablespoons vegetable oil, divided
2 tablespoons plus 1 to 2 teaspoons fresh lime juice, divided
Dash black pepper
½ cup minced white onion
2 large tomatoes, seeded and finely chopped
2 small green bell peppers, roasted, peeled and finely chopped
2 tablespoons minced cilantro
1 fresh serrano chili, minced*
Flour tortillas (8-inch diameter) (optional)

*Chili peppers can sting and irritate the skin; wear rubber gloves when handling peppers and do not touch eyes. Wash hands after handling.

1. Place steaks between pieces of plastic wrap. Pound with flat side of meat mallet to ¼-inch thickness. Cut each steak into 6-inch portions.

2. Pound 1 garlic clove with meat mallet to crush into coarse shreds. Combine with 2 tablespoons oil, 2 tablespoons lime juice and black pepper in large shallow glass baking dish. Add steaks, turning to coat with marinade. Marinate in refrigerator 30 minutes.

3. Meanwhile, prepare grill for direct grilling.**

4. Mince remaining garlic clove. Cook and stir onion and garlic in remaining 1 tablespoon oil in medium skillet over medium heat 3 to 4 minutes until onion is softened. Remove from heat.

5. Stir in tomatoes, bell peppers, cilantro and chili. Season to taste with remaining lime juice. Let stand, covered, at room temperature.

6. Remove steaks from marinade; pat dry with paper towels. Discard marinade. Grill over medium heat, uncovered, 10 to 13 minutes for medium-rare to medium or until desired doneness, turning once.

7. If not freshly made, soften and warm tortillas. Serve steaks with tomato relish, refried beans and tortillas, if desired.

Makes 4 servings

**Steaks can be cooked on lightly oiled, well-seasoned heavy griddle or large skillet. Heat over medium heat until very hot. Cook steaks in single layer on griddle 3 minutes for medium-rare or until desired doneness is reached, turning once.

Fajitas

Hot, Spicy, Tangy, Sticky Chicken

1 chicken (3½ to 4 pounds), cut up
1 cup cider vinegar
1 tablespoon Worcestershire sauce
1 tablespoon chili powder
1 teaspoon salt
1 teaspoon black pepper
1 teaspoon hot pepper sauce
¾ cup KC MASTERPIECE™ Original Barbecue Sauce

Place chicken in shallow glass dish or large heavy plastic bag. Combine vinegar, Worcestershire sauce, chili powder, salt, black pepper and hot pepper sauce in small bowl; pour over chicken pieces. Cover dish or seal bag. Marinate in refrigerator at least 4 hours, turning several times.

Oil hot grid to help prevent sticking. Place dark meat pieces on grill 10 minutes before white meat pieces (dark meat takes longer to cook). Grill chicken on a covered grill, over medium KINGSFORD® Briquets, 30 to 45 minutes, turning once or twice. Turn and baste with KC MASTERPIECE™ Original Barbecue Sauce the last 10 minutes of cooking. Remove chicken from grill; baste with barbecue sauce. Chicken is done when meat is no longer pink near bone. *Makes 4 servings*

Hot, Spicy, Tangy, Sticky Chicken

Grilled Garlic-Pepper Shrimp

⅓ cup olive oil
2 tablespoons lemon juice
1 teaspoon garlic pepper blend
20 jumbo shrimp, peeled and deveined
Lemon wedges (optional)

1. Prepare grill for direct grilling.

2. Meanwhile, combine oil, lemon juice and garlic pepper in large resealable plastic food storage bag; add shrimp. Marinate 20 to 30 minutes in refrigerator, turning bag once.

3. Thread 5 shrimp onto each of 4 skewers; discard marinade. Grill on grid over medium heat 6 minutes or until pink and opaque. Serve with lemon wedges, if desired.   *Makes 4 servings*

Hot and Spicy Spareribs

1 rack pork spareribs (3 pounds)
2 tablespoons butter or margarine
1 medium onion, finely chopped
2 cloves garlic, minced
1 can (15 ounces) tomato sauce
⅔ cup packed brown sugar
⅔ cup cider vinegar
2 tablespoons chili powder
1 tablespoon prepared mustard
½ teaspoon black pepper

Melt butter in large skillet over low heat. Add onion and garlic; cook and stir until tender. Add remaining ingredients, except ribs, and bring to a boil. Reduce heat and simmer 20 minutes, stirring occasionally.

Prepare grill with rectangular foil drip pan. Bank briquets on either side of drip pan for indirect cooking. Baste meaty side of ribs with sauce. Place ribs on grid, meaty side down, over drip pan about 6 inches above low coals; baste top side. Cover. Cook about 20 minutes; turn ribs and baste. Cook 45 minutes more or until done, basting every 10 to 15 minutes with sauce.   *Makes 3 servings*

Favorite recipe from **National Pork Board**

Grilled Garlic-Pepper Shrimp

Grilled Chicken with Southern Barbecue Sauce

   Nonstick cooking spray
½ cup chopped onion (about 1 small)
4 cloves garlic, minced
1 can (16 ounces) no-salt-added tomato sauce
¾ cup water
3 tablespoons packed light brown sugar
3 tablespoons chili sauce
2 teaspoons chili powder
2 teaspoons dried thyme leaves
2 teaspoons white Worcestershire sauce
¾ teaspoon ground red pepper
½ teaspoon ground cinnamon
½ teaspoon black pepper
6 skinless bone-in chicken breasts (2¼ pounds)

1. Spray medium nonstick skillet with cooking spray; heat over medium heat until hot. Add onion and garlic; cook and stir about 5 minutes or until tender.

2. Stir in tomato sauce, water, sugar, chili sauce, chili powder, thyme, Worcestershire sauce, red pepper, cinnamon and black pepper; heat to a boil. Reduce heat to low and simmer, uncovered, 30 minutes or until mixture is reduced to about 1½ cups. Reserve ¾ cup sauce for basting.

3. Meanwhile, prepare grill for direct grilling.

4. Grill chicken, on covered grill over medium-hot coals 40 to 45 minutes or until chicken is no longer pink in center and juices run clear, turning chicken several times and basting occasionally with reserved sauce.

5. Heat remaining sauce in skillet over medium heat until hot; spoon over chicken. Serve with potatoes and additional vegetables, if desired.

Makes 6 servings

Grilled Chicken with Southern Barbecue Sauce

Marinated Italian Sausage and Peppers

½ cup olive oil
¼ cup red wine vinegar
2 tablespoons chopped fresh parsley
1 tablespoon dried oregano leaves
2 cloves garlic, crushed
1 teaspoon salt
1 teaspoon black pepper
4 hot or sweet Italian sausage links
1 large onion, cut into slices
1 large bell pepper, cut into quarters
Horseradish-Mustard Spread (recipe follows)

1. Combine oil, vinegar, parsley, oregano, garlic, salt and black pepper in small bowl. Place sausages, onion and bell pepper in large resealable plastic food storage bag; pour oil mixture into bag. Close bag securely, turning to coat. Marinate in refrigerator 1 to 2 hours.

2. Prepare Horseradish-Mustard Spread; set aside. Prepare grill for direct cooking. Drain sausages, onion and bell pepper; reserve marinade.

3. Grill sausages, covered, 4 to 5 minutes. Turn sausages and place onion and bell pepper on grid. Brush sausages and vegetables with reserved marinade. Grill, covered, 5 minutes or until vegetables are crisp-tender, turning vegetables halfway through grilling time. Serve sausages, onions and bell peppers Horseradish-Mustard Spread.

Makes 4 servings

Horseradish-Mustard Spread

3 tablespoons mayonnaise
1 tablespoon chopped fresh parsley
1 tablespoon prepared horseradish
1 tablespoon Dijon mustard
2 teaspoons garlic powder
1 teaspoon black pepper

Combine all ingredients in small bowl; mix well.

Makes about ½ cup

Marinated Italian Sausage and Peppers

Shish Kabobs

½ cup **CRISCO® Oil**
½ cup **chopped onion**
¼ cup **red wine vinegar**
¼ cup **ketchup**
2 tablespoons **Worcestershire sauce**
2 cloves **garlic, peeled and mashed**
1 teaspoon **salt**
½ teaspoon **chopped fresh oregano or rosemary**
¼ teaspoon **black pepper**
3 pounds **lamb or beef, cut into 1-inch cubes**
   Green bell pepper squares
   Small onions
   Tomato wedges or cherry tomatoes
   Mushrooms

Combine first 9 ingredients in a large bowl. Add meat and stir to coat with sauce. Cover and refrigerate overnight.

Alternately skewer cubes of meat with desired combination of bell pepper squares, small onions, tomatoes and mushrooms.

Place kabobs on grid about 5 inches above hot coals. Turn often until meat reaches desired doneness.   *Makes about 8 servings*

Hint: To broil, preheat broiler. Place kabobs about 5 inches from the broiler. Broil about 5 minutes. Turn and broil about 5 minutes longer or until meat is done.

Shish Kabobs

California Turkey Burgers

1 pound ground turkey
½ cup finely chopped cilantro
⅓ cup plain dry bread crumbs
3 tablespoons *French's*® Classic Yellow® Mustard
1 egg, beaten
½ teaspoon salt
¼ teaspoon black pepper
8 thin slices (3 ounces) Monterey Jack cheese
½ red or yellow bell pepper, seeded and cut into rings
4 hamburger buns

1. Combine turkey, cilantro, bread crumbs, mustard, egg, salt and pepper in large bowl. Shape into 4 patties, pressing firmly.

2. Place patties on oiled grid. Grill over high heat 15 minutes or until no longer pink in center (160°F). Top burgers with cheese during last few minutes of grilling. Grill pepper rings 2 minutes. To serve, place burgers on buns and top with pepper rings. Serve with additional mustard, if desired.   *Makes 4 servings*

Prep Time: 15 minutes
Cook Time: 15 minutes

California Turkey Burger

Grilled Chicken Caesar Salad

1 pound boneless skinless chicken breasts
½ cup extra-virgin olive oil
3 tablespoons fresh lemon juice
2 teaspoons anchovy paste
2 cloves garlic, minced
½ teaspoon salt
½ teaspoon black pepper
6 cups torn romaine lettuce leaves
4 plum tomatoes, quartered
¼ cup grated Parmesan cheese
1 cup purchased garlic croutons

1. Place chicken in large resealable plastic food storage bag. Combine oil, lemon juice, anchovy paste, garlic, salt and pepper in small bowl. Reserve ⅓ cup of marinade; cover and refrigerate until serving. Pour remaining marinade over chicken in bag. Seal bag tightly, turning to coat. Marinate in refrigerator at least 1 hour or up to 4 hours, turning occasionally.

2. Combine lettuce, tomatoes and cheese in large bowl. Cover; refrigerate until serving.

3. Prepare grill for direct cooking.

4. Drain chicken, pouring marinade into small saucepan. Bring marinade to a boil; boil 1 minute.

5. Place chicken on grid. Grill chicken, on covered grill, over medium coals 10 to 12 minutes or until chicken is no longer pink in center, brushing with marinade after 5 minutes and turning halfway through grilling time. Discard remaining marinade. Cool chicken slightly.

6. Slice warm chicken crosswise into ½-inch-wide strips; add chicken and croutons to lettuce mixture in bowl. Drizzle with ⅓ cup reserved marinade; toss to coat well.

Makes 4 servings

Note: Chicken can also be refrigerated until cold before slicing.

Grilled Chicken Caesar Salad

Maple Francheezies

Mustard Spread (recipe follows)
¼ **cup maple syrup**
2 **teaspoons garlic powder**
1 **teaspoon black pepper**
½ **teaspoon ground nutmeg**
4 **slices bacon**
4 **jumbo hot dogs**
4 **hot dog buns, split**
½ **cup (2 ounces) shredded Cheddar cheese**

1. Prepare Mustard Spread; set aside.

2. Prepare grill for direct cooking.

3. Combine maple syrup, garlic powder, pepper and nutmeg in small bowl. Brush syrup mixture onto bacon slices. Wrap 1 slice bacon around each hot dog.

4. Brush hot dogs with remaining syrup mixture. Place hot dogs on grid. Grill, covered, over medium-high heat 8 minutes or until bacon is crisp and hot dogs are heated through, turning halfway through grilling time. Place hot dogs in buns, top with Mustard Spread and cheese.   *Makes 4 servings*

Mustard Spread

½ **cup prepared yellow mustard**
1 **tablespoon finely chopped onion**
1 **tablespoon diced tomato**
1 **tablespoon chopped fresh parsley**
1 **teaspoon garlic powder**
½ **teaspoon black pepper**

Combine all ingredients in small bowl; mix well.   *Makes about ¾ cup*

Maple Francheezie

All-American Onion Burger

1 pound ground beef
2 tablespoons *French's*® **Worcestershire Sauce**
1⅓ cups *French's*® **French Fried Onions, divided**
½ teaspoon garlic salt
¼ teaspoon ground black pepper
4 hamburger rolls

Combine beef, Worcestershire, ⅔ cup French Fried Onions, garlic salt and pepper. Form into 4 patties. Place patties on grid. Grill over hot coals about 10 minutes or until meat thermometer inserted into beef reaches 160°F, turning once. Top with remaining ⅔ cup onions. Serve on rolls.   *Makes 4 servings*

Luscious Oniony Cheeseburger: Place 1 slice cheese on each burger before topping with French Fried Onions.

Tangy Western Burger: Top each burger with 1 tablespoon barbecue sauce and 1 strip crisp bacon before topping with French Fried Onions.

California Burger: Combine 2 tablespoons each mayonnaise, sour cream and *French's*® Bold n' Spicy Brown Mustard in small bowl; spoon over burgers. Top each burger with avocado slices, sprouts and French Fried Onions.

Salisbury Steak Burger: Prepare 1 package brown gravy mix according to directions. Stir in 1 can (4 ounces) drained sliced mushrooms. Spoon over burgers and top with French Fried Onions.

Pizza Burger: Top each burger with pizza sauce, mozzarella cheese and French Fried Onions.

Chili Burger: Combine 1 can (15 ounces) chili without beans, 2 tablespoons *Frank's RedHot* Sauce and 2 teaspoons each chili powder and ground cumin. Cook until heated through. Spoon over burgers and top with French Fried Onions.

Prep Time: 10 minutes
Cook Time: 10 minutes

California Burger

Grilled Chicken with Chili Beer Baste

2 tablespoons vegetable oil
1 small onion, chopped
1 clove garlic, minced
½ cup ketchup
2 tablespoons brown sugar
2 teaspoons chili powder
2 chipotle peppers in adobo sauce, minced
1 teaspoon dry mustard
½ teaspoon salt
½ teaspoon black pepper
3 bottles (12 ounces each) pilsner beer, divided
½ cup tomato juice
¼ cup Worcestershire sauce
1 tablespoon lemon juice
2 whole chickens (about 3½ pounds each), cut up

1. To make Chili Beer Baste, heat oil in 2-quart saucepan over medium heat. Add onion and garlic; cook until onion is tender. Combine ketchup, brown sugar, chili powder, chipotle peppers, mustard, salt and pepper in medium bowl. Add 1 bottle of beer, tomato juice, Worcestershire sauce and lemon juice; whisk until well blended. Pour into saucepan with onion and garlic. Bring to a simmer; cook until sauce has thickened slightly and is reduced to about 2 cups. Let cool. Refrigerate overnight.

2. Place chicken pieces in 2 large resealable plastic food storage bags. Pour remaining 2 bottles beer over chicken in each bag; seal bags. Refrigerate 8 hours or overnight.

3. Prepare grill for direct grilling; grease grid. Remove chickens from marinade; drain and discard marinade. Place chicken leg and thigh quarters on hottest part of grid 4 to 6 inches above bed of coals (coals should be evenly covered with gray ashes); place breast pieces above medium-hot coals (toward edge of coals). Grill, turning occasionally, 25 to 30 minutes.

4. Remove Chili Beer Baste from refrigerator; reserve 1 cup. Brush chicken generously with remaining basting sauce during last 10 minutes of cooking. Internal temperature should reach 180°F for dark meat and 170°F for breast meat. Serve chicken with warmed reserved baste. *Makes 8 servings*

Grilled Chicken with Chili Beer Baste

Shrimp on the Barbie

1 pound large raw shrimp, shelled and deveined
1 *each* red and yellow bell peppers, seeded and cut into 1-inch
    chunks
4 slices lime (optional)
½ cup prepared smoky-flavor barbecue sauce
2 tablespoons *French's*® Worcestershire Sauce
2 tablespoons *Frank's*® *RedHot*® Original Cayenne Pepper Sauce
1 clove garlic, minced

Thread shrimp, peppers and lime, if desired, alternately onto metal skewers. Combine barbecue sauce, Worcestershire, **Frank's RedHot** Sauce and garlic in small bowl; mix well. Brush on skewers.

Place skewers on grid, reserving remaining sauce mixture. Grill over hot coals 15 minutes or until shrimp turn pink, turning and basting often with sauce mixture. (Do not baste during last 5 minutes of cooking.) Serve warm.   *Makes 4 servings*

Prep Time: 10 minutes
Cook Time: 15 minutes

Shrimp on the Barbie

Sizzling Franks with Grilled Corn and Black Beans

2 ears fresh corn, shucked
2 tablespoons vegetable or olive oil, divided
1 package (12 ounces) HEBREW NATIONAL® Beef Franks, Reduced Fat Beef Franks or 97% Fat Free Beef Franks
½ cup chopped red or yellow onion
½ cup seeded chopped red bell pepper
1 can (16 ounces) black beans, drained
½ cup prepared chunky salsa
Chopped cilantro, for garnish

Prepare barbecue grill for direct cooking. Brush corn with 1 tablespoon oil. Place corn and franks on grid over medium-hot coals. Grill 10 to 12 minutes on uncovered grill or until corn is tender and franks are heated through.

Heat remaining 1 tablespoon oil in medium saucepan over medium-high heat. Add onion; cook 3 minutes. Add bell pepper; cook 2 minutes. Add beans and salsa. Cover; simmer 5 minutes or until heated through.

Cut corn from cobs; discard cobs. Stir corn into bean mixture. Transfer bean mixture to serving plates. Top bean mixture with franks. Garnish with cilantro, if desired.

Makes 6 servings

Sizzling Franks with Grilled Corn and Black Beans

The Meat Lover's Grill

Maple-Mustard-Glazed Spareribs

 4 pounds pork spareribs
 ½ teaspoon salt
 ½ teaspoon pickling spices*
 2 teaspoons vegetable oil
 1 small onion, coarsely chopped
 ½ cup maple-flavored syrup
 ¼ cup cider vinegar
 2 tablespoons water
 1 tablespoon Dijon mustard
    Dash salt
 ¼ teaspoon black pepper

Pickling spices is a blend of seasonings used for pickling foods. It can include allspice, bay leaves, cardamom, coriander, cinnamon, cloves, ginger, mustard seeds and/or pepper. Most supermarkets carry prepackaged pickling spices in the spice aisle.

Sprinkle spareribs with ½ teaspoon salt. Place pickling spices in several thicknesses of cheesecloth; tie up to make a bouquet garni. Set aside. For glaze, heat oil in small saucepan; add onion. Cook and stir until tender. Add bouquet garni. Stir in syrup, vinegar, water, mustard, dash salt and pepper. Bring to a boil over medium-high heat; reduce heat to low and simmer 20 minutes. Discard bouquet garni.

Prepare grill with rectangular foil drip pan. Bank briquets on either side of drip pan for indirect cooking. Place ribs on grid over drip pan. Grill, on covered grill, over low coals 1½ hours or until ribs are tender, turning and basting occasionally with glaze. (Do not baste during last 5 minutes of grilling.) *Makes 4 servings*

Prep Time: 20 minutes
Cooking Time: 90 minutes

Favorite recipe from **National Pork Board**

Maple-Mustard-Glazed Spareribs

Asian Grilled Steaks with Spicy Herb Sauce

⅔ cup CRISCO® Oil
3 tablespoons sugar
3 tablespoons cooking sherry
1 tablespoon plus 1½ teaspoons minced garlic
1 tablespoon dark sesame oil
1 teaspoon red pepper flakes
½ teaspoon salt
6 (1-inch-thick) strip steaks
Salt and black pepper, to taste

Spicy Herb Sauce
1 cup chopped cilantro, including stems
⅓ cup CRISCO® Oil
1 tablespoon fresh lime juice
3 tablespoons soy sauce
1½ teaspoons minced garlic
½ teaspoon dark sesame oil
½ teaspoon minced jalapeño pepper*

Jalapeño peppers can sting and irritate the skin; wear rubber gloves when handling peppers and do not touch eyes. Wash hands after handling.

Stir together CRISCO® Oil, sugar, sherry, garlic, sesame oil, pepper flakes and salt in a 13×9-inch baking dish. Stir until sugar is dissolved. Season steaks with salt and pepper. Add steaks, turning once to coat. Marinate for 1 hour, turning once.

To make Spicy Herb Sauce, stir together cilantro, CRISCO® Oil, lime juice, soy sauce, garlic, sesame oil and jalapeño; set aside.

Preheat grill for direct grilling.

Remove steaks from marinade. Discard marinade. Cook steaks on a medium-hot grill for 3 to 4 minutes per side for medium-rare or until desired doneness. Top each steak with sauce.   *Makes 6 servings*

Asian Grilled Steak with Spicy Herb Sauce

Sausage & Wilted Spinach Salad

¼ cup sherry vinegar or white wine vinegar
1 teaspoon whole mustard seeds, crushed
½ teaspoon salt
¼ teaspoon black pepper
2 ears corn, husked
1 large red onion, cut into ¾-inch-thick slices
4 tablespoons extra-virgin olive oil, divided
12 ounces smoked turkey, chicken or pork sausage links, such as
       Polish, andouille or New Mexico style, cut in half lengthwise
2 cloves garlic, minced
10 cups lightly packed spinach leaves, torn
1 large avocado, peeled and cubed

Combine vinegar, mustard seeds, salt and pepper; set dressing aside. Brush corn and onion with 1 tablespoon oil. Insert wooden picks into onion slices from edges to prevent separating into rings. (Soak wooden picks in hot water 15 minutes to prevent burning.) Grill sausage, corn and onion over medium KINGSFORD® Briquets 6 to 10 minutes until vegetables are crisp-tender and sausage is hot, turning several times. Cut corn kernels from cobs; chop onion and slice sausage. Heat remaining 3 tablespoons oil in small skillet over medium heat. Add garlic; cook and stir 1 minute. Toss spinach, avocado, sausage, corn, onion and dressing in large bowl. Drizzle hot oil mixture over salad; toss and serve immediately.   *Makes 4 servings*

According to the Dictionary of American Slang, "barbecue" can refer to a sexy young woman.

Sausage & Wilted Spinach Salad

Marinated Grilled Lamb Chops

8 well-trimmed lamb loin chops, 1 inch thick (about 2¼ pounds)
3 cloves garlic, minced
2 tablespoons chopped fresh rosemary *or* 2 teaspoons dried
    rosemary, crushed
2 tablespoons chopped fresh mint leaves *or* 2 teaspoons dried mint
    leaves
¾ cup dry red wine
⅓ cup butter or margarine, softened
¼ teaspoon salt
¼ teaspoon black pepper
    Fresh mint leaves for garnish

1. To marinate, place chops in large resealable plastic food storage bag. Combine garlic, rosemary and chopped mint in small bowl. Combine ½ of garlic mixture and wine in glass measuring cup. Pour wine mixture over chops in bag. Close bag securely; turn to coat. Marinate chops in refrigerator at least 2 hours or up to 4 hours, turning occasionally.

2. Add butter, salt and pepper to remaining garlic mixture; mix well. Spoon onto center of sheet of plastic wrap. Using plastic wrap as a guide, shape butter mixture into 4×1½-inch log. Wrap securely in plastic wrap; refrigerate until ready to serve.

3. Prepare grill for direct cooking. Drain chops, discarding marinade. Place chops on grid. Grill, on covered grill, over medium coals about 9 minutes or until instant-read thermometer inserted into chops registers 160°F for medium or to desired doneness, turning once.

4. Cut butter log crosswise into 8 (½-inch) slices. To serve, top each chop with slice of seasoned butter. Garnish, if desired. *Makes 4 servings*

Marinated Grilled Lamb Chops

Lamb Chops with Cranberry-Orange Salsa

**1 medium orange, sectioned and chopped *or* ½ cup canned
        mandarin oranges, chopped**
¼ cup finely chopped onion
¼ cup chopped green chilies, drained
¼ cup dried cranberries
¼ cup orange marmalade
1 tablespoon finely chopped cilantro
1 tablespoon vinegar
2 tablespoons orange juice
1 teaspoon Worcestershire sauce
8 American lamb loin chops, 1 inch thick (about 2 pounds)

For salsa, combine orange, onion, chilies, cranberries, marmalade, cilantro and vinegar. Cover; chill several hours. Combine orange juice and Worcestershire. Brush lamb with juice mixture. Grill over medium coals or broil 4 inches from heat source for 5 minutes. Turn and grill 4 to 6 minutes longer or to medium doneness. Serve with salsa. *Makes 4 servings*

Favorite recipe from **American Lamb Council**

Lamb Chops with Cranberry-Orange Salsa

Grilled Caribbean Steak with Tropical Fruit Rice

    1 (1½-pound) flank steak
 1¼ cups orange juice, divided
   ¼ cup soy sauce
    1 teaspoon ground ginger
    1 can (8 ounces) pineapple chunks in juice
   ¼ teaspoon ground allspice
    1 cup UNCLE BEN'S® ORIGINAL CONVERTED® Brand Rice
    1 can (11 ounces) mandarin orange segments, drained

1. Place steak in large resealable plastic food storage bag. In small bowl, combine ¼ cup orange juice, soy sauce and ginger; pour over steak. Seal bag, turning to coat steak with marinade. Refrigerate steak, turning bag occasionally, at least 8 or up to 24 hours.

2. Drain pineapple, reserving juice. Combine remaining 1 cup orange juice and pineapple juice in 1-quart glass measure; add enough water to make 2¼ cups liquid.

3. In medium saucepan, combine juice mixture, allspice and salt to taste. Bring to a boil; stir in rice. Cover; reduce heat to low and simmer 20 minutes. Remove from heat and let stand, covered, 5 minutes.

4. Meanwhile, remove steak from marinade; discard marinade. Grill steak over direct medium or high heat 7 minutes on each side for medium or until desired doneness. Cut steak diagonally across the grain into thin slices.

5. Place rice in serving bowl. Stir in pineapple and oranges. Serve with steak.

Makes 6 servings

Serving Suggestion: For an authentic Caribbean touch, add 1 cup diced peeled mango to rice with pineapple chunks and oranges.

Grilled Caribbean Steak with Tropical Fruit Rice

Barbecue Pork Kabobs

½ cup ketchup
¼ cup white vinegar
¼ cup vegetable oil
1 tablespoon brown sugar
1 teaspoon dry mustard
1 clove garlic *or* ½ teaspoon garlic powder
½ teaspoon salt
½ teaspoon Worcestershire sauce
¼ teaspoon black pepper
¼ teaspoon hot pepper sauce (optional)
4 boneless pork chops, cut into 1½-inch cubes
2 green bell peppers, cut into chunks
2 onions, cut into chunks
Skewers

1. Combine ketchup, vinegar, oil, brown sugar, dry mustard, garlic, salt, Worcestershire, black pepper and hot pepper sauce, if desired, in large resealable plastic food storage bag; mix well. Reserve ¼ cup marinade for basting. Add pork; seal bag. Marinate in refrigerator at least 1 hour.

2. Remove pork from marinade; discard used marinade. Alternately thread pork, bell peppers and onions onto skewers. Grill skewers 15 to 20 minutes or until pork is barely pink in center, turning once and basting often with reserved ¼ cup marinade. *Do not baste during last 5 minutes of cooking.* Discard any remaining marinade.

Makes 4 servings

Serving Suggestion: Serve over red beans and rice.

Hint: If using wooden skewers, soak them in water for 30 minutes before using to prevent scorching.

Barbecue Pork Kabobs

Steakhouse London Broil

1 package KNORR® Recipe Classics™ Roasted Garlic Herb or French Onion Soup, Dip and Recipe Mix
⅓ cup BERTOLLI® Olive Oil
2 tablespoons red wine vinegar
1 (1½- to 2-pound) beef top round steak (for London Broil) or flank steak

• In large plastic food bag or 13×9-inch glass baking dish, blend recipe mix, oil and vinegar.

• Add steak, turning to coat. Close bag, or cover, and marinate in refrigerator 30 minutes to 3 hours.

• Remove meat from marinade, discarding marinade. Grill or broil, turning occasionally, until desired doneness.

• Slice meat thinly across the grain.   *Makes 6 to 8 servings*

Garlic Chicken: Substitute 6 to 8 boneless chicken breasts or 3 to 4 pounds bone-in chicken pieces for steak. Marinate as directed. Grill boneless chicken breasts 6 minutes or bone-in chicken pieces 20 minutes or until chicken is thoroughly cooked.

Prep Time: 5 minutes
Marinate Time: 30 minutes to 3 hours
Grill Time: 20 minutes

Steakhouse London Broil

Grilled Lamb Fajitas

3 tablespoons olive oil
3 tablespoons tequila or orange juice
2 tablespoons fresh lime juice
1 teaspoon ground cumin
1 teaspoon chili powder
1 teaspoon dried oregano leaves, crushed
½ teaspoon salt
¼ teaspoon black pepper
¼ teaspoon red pepper flakes, crushed
¼ cup chopped fresh cilantro
1½ pounds lean American lamb leg steaks, cut 1 inch thick
6 green onions
3 fresh poblano or ancho chilies (optional)
1 red bell pepper, halved and seeded
1 green bell pepper, halved and seeded
1 yellow bell pepper, halved and seeded
12 medium flour tortillas, warmed
Salsa

For marinade, in small bowl combine oil, tequila, lime juice, cumin, chili powder, oregano, salt, black pepper, red pepper flakes and cilantro. Place lamb in glass dish. Pour marinade over lamb; cover and refrigerate 4 to 6 hours.

Ignite coals in grill; allow to burn until bright red and covered with gray ash. Drain lamb; discard marinade. Grill lamb, onions, chilies and red, green and yellow peppers 4 inches from coals. Cook steaks 5 to 6 minutes per side for medium-rare or to desired degree of doneness. Turn vegetables frequently until cooked. Slice lamb steaks and vegetables into ¼-inch-thick slices. Serve on tortillas, top with salsa and roll up.

Makes 12 servings

Favorite recipe from **American Lamb Council**

Grilled Lamb Fajitas

Herb Orange Pork Chops

1½ **cups orange juice**
¼ **cup vegetable oil, divided**
1½ **teaspoons salt**
1½ **teaspoons freshly ground black pepper**
2 **cloves garlic, crushed**
1 **teaspoon dried thyme leaves**
4 **pork loin chops, cut ¾ inch thick**
½ **cup thinly sliced green onions**
1 **teaspoon grated fresh orange peel**

1. Combine orange juice, 3 tablespoons oil, salt, pepper, garlic and thyme in small bowl. Place chops and ¾ cup marinade in large resealable plastic food storage bag; seal bag. Marinate in refrigerator at least 1 hour. Reserve remaining 1 cup marinade.

2. Remove chops from marinade; discard bag and marinade. Grill chops about 10 to 15 minutes or until barely pink in center, turning halfway through grilling time.

3. Heat remaining 1 tablespoon oil in large skillet. Add onions and orange peel; cook over medium heat 1 minute. Stir in reserved marinade. Reduce heat to low; cook until reduced by half. Serve over chops. *Makes 4 servings*

Serving Suggestion: Serve with fresh fruit.

Herbed Orange Pork Chop

Guadalajara Beef and Salsa

1 bottle (12 ounces) Mexican dark beer*
¼ cup soy sauce
2 cloves garlic, minced
1 teaspoon ground cumin
1 teaspoon chili powder
1 teaspoon hot pepper sauce
4 boneless beef sirloin or top loin strip steaks (4 to 6 ounces each)
   Salt and black pepper
   Red, green and yellow bell peppers, cut lengthwise into quarters,
     seeded (optional)
   Salsa (recipe follows)
   Flour tortillas (optional)
   Lime wedges

*Substitute any beer for Mexican dark beer.

Combine beer, soy sauce, garlic, cumin, chili powder and hot pepper sauce in large shallow glass dish or large heavy plastic food storage bag. Add beef; cover dish or close bag. Marinate in refrigerator up to 12 hours, turning beef several times. Remove beef from marinade; discard marinade. Season with salt and black pepper.

Oil hot grid to help prevent sticking. Grill beef and bell peppers, if desired, on covered grill, over medium KINGSFORD® Briquets, 8 to 12 minutes, turning once. Beef should be of medium doneness and peppers should be tender. Serve with salsa, tortillas, if desired, and lime wedges. *Makes 4 servings*

SALSA: Combine 2 cups coarsely chopped tomatoes, 2 sliced green onions, 1 tablespoon olive oil, 2 to 4 teaspoons lime juice, 1 minced clove garlic and 1 to 2 teaspoons minced jalapeño or serrano chili pepper in medium bowl. Season with ½ teaspoon salt, ½ teaspoon sugar and ¼ teaspoon black pepper. Stir in 8 to 10 sprigs chopped fresh cilantro, if desired. Adjust seasonings to taste, adding more lime juice or chili pepper, if desired.

Guadalajara Beef

Wine & Rosemary Lamb Skewers

1 cup dry red wine
¼ cup olive oil
3 cloves garlic, cut into slivers
1 tablespoon chopped fresh thyme *or* 1 teaspoon dried thyme leaves, crumbled
1 tablespoon chopped fresh rosemary *or* 1 teaspoon dried rosemary leaves, crumbled
2 pounds boneless lamb, cut into 1-inch cubes
Salt and black pepper
4 or 5 sprigs fresh rosemary (optional)
Grilled Bread (recipe follows)

Combine wine, oil, garlic, thyme and rosemary in a shallow glass dish or large heavy plastic food storage bag. Add lamb; cover dish or close bag. Marinate lamb in the refrigerator up to 12 hours, turning several times. Remove lamb from marinade; discard marinade. Thread lamb onto 6 long metal skewers. Season to taste with salt and pepper.

Oil hot grid to help prevent sticking. Grill lamb, on a covered grill, over medium KINGSFORD® Briquets, 8 to 12 minutes, turning once or twice. Remove grill cover and throw rosemary onto coals the last 4 to 5 minutes of cooking, if desired. Move skewers to side of grid to keep warm while bread is toasting. Garnish, if desired.

Makes 6 servings

Grilled Bread

¼ cup olive oil
2 tablespoons red wine vinegar
1 French bread baguette (about 12 inches long), sliced lengthwise, then cut into pieces
Salt and freshly ground black pepper

Mix oil and vinegar in cup; brush over cut surfaces of bread. Season lightly with salt and pepper. Grill bread cut side down, on an uncovered grill, over medium KINGSFORD® Briquets until lightly toasted.

Makes 6 servings

Wine & Rosemary Lamb Skewers

Steak with Parmesan-Grilled Vegetables

2 well-trimmed beef T-bone or Porterhouse steaks, cut 1 inch thick (about 2 pounds)
1 tablespoon crushed garlic
2 teaspoons dried basil leaves
1 teaspoon black pepper
¼ cup grated Parmesan cheese
2 tablespoons olive oil
2 tablespoons red wine vinegar
2 medium red or yellow bell peppers, each cut lengthwise into quarters
1 large red onion, cut crosswise into ½-inch slices
Salt

1. Combine garlic, basil and black pepper in small bowl; mix well. Remove 4 teaspoons seasoning; press onto both sides of steaks.

2. Add cheese, oil and vinegar to remaining seasoning, mixing well; set aside.

3. Place steaks in center of grid over medium coals; arrange vegetables around steaks. Grill steaks uncovered 14 to 16 minutes for medium-rare to medium doneness, turning occasionally. Grill peppers 12 to 15 minutes and onion 15 to 20 minutes or until tender, turning both once. Brush vegetables with cheese mixture during last 10 minutes of grilling.

4. Season steaks to taste with salt. Trim fat from steaks; remove bones. Carve steaks crosswise into thick slices; serve with vegetables.   *Makes 4 servings*

Favorite recipe from **North Dakota Beef Commission**

Steak with Parmesan-Grilled Vegetables

Spicy Smoked Beef Ribs

Wood chunks or chips for smoking
4 to 6 pounds beef back ribs, cut into 3 to 4 rib pieces
Black pepper
1⅓ cups barbecue sauce, divided
2 teaspoons hot pepper sauce or chili sauce
Beer at room temperature or hot tap water

1. Prepare grill for indirect grilling. Soak 4 wood chunks or several handfuls of wood chips in water; drain.

2. Spread ribs on baking sheet or tray; season with pepper. Combine barbecue sauce and hot pepper sauce. Brush ribs with half of sauce. Marinate in the refrigerator 30 minutes to 1 hour.

3. Arrange low coals on each side of rectangular metal or foil drip pan. (Since the ribs have been brushed with sauce before cooking, low heat is needed to keep them moist.) Pour in beer to fill pan half full. Add soaked wood (all the chunks; part of chips) to fire.

4. Oil hot grid to help prevent sticking. Place ribs on grid, meaty side up, directly above drip pan. Cook ribs, on covered grill, about 1 hour, brushing remaining sauce over ribs 2 or 3 times during cooking. If grill has thermometer, maintain cooking temperature between 250°F to 275°F. Add a few more briquets after 30 minutes, or as necessary, to maintain constant temperature. Add more soaked wood chips every 30 minutes, if necessary. Serve with grilled corn-on-the-cob, if desired.   *Makes 4 to 6 servings*

An average fire uses 3 to 4 pounds of charcoal.

Spicy Smoked Beef Ribs

Spice-Rubbed Beef Brisket

2 cups hickory chips
1 teaspoon salt
1 teaspoon paprika
1 teaspoon chili powder
1 teaspoon garlic pepper
1 beef brisket (3 to 3½ pounds)
¼ cup beer or beef broth
1 tablespoon Worcestershire sauce
1 tablespoon balsamic vinegar
1 teaspoon olive oil
¼ teaspoon dry mustard
6 ears corn, cut into 2-inch pieces
12 small new potatoes
6 carrots, cut into 2-inch pieces
2 green bell peppers, cut into 2-inch squares
6 tablespoons lemon juice
6 tablespoons water
1½ teaspoons salt-free dried Italian seasoning

1. Cover hickory chips with water and soak 30 minutes. Prepare grill for indirect grilling. Bank briquets on either side of water-filled drip pan.

2. Combine salt, paprika, chili powder and garlic pepper. Rub spice mixture onto both sides of brisket; loosely cover with foil and set aside. Combine beer, Worcestershire sauce, vinegar, oil and dry mustard; set aside.

3. Drain hickory chips; sprinkle ½ cup over coals. Place brisket on grid directly over drip pan; grill on covered grill over medium coals 30 minutes. Baste with reserved beer mixture; turn over every 30 minutes for 3 hours or until meat thermometer reaches 160°F when inserted into thickest part of brisket. Add 4 to 9 briquets and ¼ cup hickory chips to each side of fire every hour or as needed.

4. Alternately thread vegetables onto metal skewers. Combine lemon juice, water and Italian seasoning; brush onto vegetables. Grill vegetables with brisket 20 to 25 minutes or until tender, turning once.

5. Remove brisket to cutting board; tent loosely with foil and let stand 10 minutes before carving. Remove excess fat. Serve beef with vegetable kabobs. Garnish as desired.
Makes 12 servings

Spice-Rubbed Beef Brisket

Marinated Flank Steak with Pineapple

1 can (15¼ ounces) DEL MONTE® Sliced Pineapple In Its Own Juice
¼ cup teriyaki sauce
2 tablespoons honey
1 pound beef flank steak

1. Drain pineapple, reserving 2 tablespoons juice. Set aside pineapple for later use.

2. Combine reserved juice, teriyaki sauce and honey in shallow 2-quart dish; mix well. Add meat; turn to coat. Cover and refrigerate at least 30 minutes or overnight.

3. Remove meat from marinade, reserving marinade. Grill meat over hot coals (or broil), brushing occasionally with reserved marinade. Cook about 4 minutes on each side for rare; about 5 minutes on each side for medium; or about 6 minutes on each side for well done. During last 4 minutes of cooking, grill pineapple until heated through.

4. Slice meat across grain; serve with pineapple. Garnish, if desired.

Makes 4 servings

Note: Marinade that has come into contact with raw meat must be discarded or boiled for several minutes before serving with cooked food.

Prep and Marinate Time: 35 minutes
Cook Time: 10 minutes

Marinated Flank Steak with Pineapple

Rosemary-Crusted Leg of Lamb

¼ cup Dijon mustard
2 large cloves garlic, minced
1 boneless butterflied leg of lamb (sirloin half, about 2½ pounds), well trimmed
3 tablespoons chopped fresh rosemary *or* 1 tablespoon dried rosemary leaves
Fresh rosemary sprigs (optional)
Mint jelly (optional)

1. Prepare grill for direct cooking.

2. Combine mustard and garlic in small bowl; spread half of mixture over one side of lamb. Sprinkle with half of chopped rosemary; pat into mustard mixture. Turn lamb over; repeat with remaining mustard mixture and rosemary. Insert heatproof meat thermometer into center of thickest part of lamb.

3. Place lamb on grid. Grill, covered, over medium coals 35 to 40 minutes or until thermometer registers 160°F for medium or until desired doneness is reached, turning every 10 minutes.

4. Meanwhile, soak rosemary sprigs in water, if desired. Place rosemary sprigs directly on coals during last 10 minutes of grilling.

5. Transfer lamb to carving board; tent with foil. Let stand 10 minutes before carving into thin slices. Serve with mint jelly, if desired. *Makes 8 servings*

Rosemary-Crusted Leg of Lamb

The Bird on the Grill

Carolina-Style Barbecue Chicken

2 pounds boneless skinless chicken breast halves or thighs
¾ cup packed light brown sugar, divided
¾ cup French's® Classic Yellow® Mustard
½ cup cider vinegar
¼ cup Frank's® RedHot® Original Cayenne Pepper Sauce
2 tablespoons vegetable oil
2 tablespoons French's® Worcestershire Sauce
½ teaspoon salt
¼ teaspoon black pepper

1. Place chicken in large resealable plastic food storage bag. Combine ½ cup brown sugar, mustard, vinegar, **Frank's RedHot** Sauce, oil, Worcestershire, salt and pepper in 4-cup measure; mix well. Pour 1 cup mustard mixture over chicken. Seal bag; marinate in refrigerator 1 hour or overnight.

2. Pour remaining mustard mixture into small saucepan. Stir in remaining ¼ cup sugar. Bring to a boil. Reduce heat; simmer 5 minutes or until sugar dissolves and mixture thickens slightly, stirring often. Reserve for serving sauce.

3. Place chicken on well-oiled grid, reserving marinade. Grill over high heat 10 to 15 minutes or until chicken is no longer pink in center, turning and basting once with marinade. *Do not baste during last 5 minutes of cooking.* Discard any remaining marinade. Serve chicken with reserved sauce. *Makes 8 servings*

Prep Time: 15 minutes
Marinate Time: 1 hour
Cook Time: 10 minutes

Carolina-Style Barbecue Chicken

Butterflied Cornish Game Hens

2 Cornish game hens* (about 3 pounds)
Olive oil cooking spray
Seasoned salt
Ground black pepper
½ cup _French's_® Honey Dijon Mustard
Grilled vegetables (optional)

You can substitute 3 pounds chicken parts (skinned, if desired) for the game hens.

Remove neck and giblets from hens; discard. Wash hens and pat dry. Place 1 hen, breast side down, on cutting board. With kitchen shears or sharp knife, cut along one side of backbone, cutting as close to bone as possible. Cut down other side of backbone; remove backbone. Spread bird open and turn breast side up, pressing to flatten. Repeat with remaining hen.

To keep drumsticks flat, make small slit through skin with point of knife between thigh and breast. Push end of leg through slit. Repeat on other side of bird and with remaining hen. Coat both sides of hens with olive oil cooking spray. Sprinkle with seasoned salt and pepper. Generously brush mustard onto both sides of hens.

Place hens, skin sides up, on oiled grid. Grill over medium-high coals 35 to 45 minutes until meat is no longer pink near bone and juices run clear, turning and basting often with remaining mustard. (Do not baste during last 10 minutes of cooking.) Serve with grilled vegetables, if desired. *Makes 4 servings*

Prep Time: 15 minutes
Cook Time: 45 minutes

Butterflied Cornish Game Hens

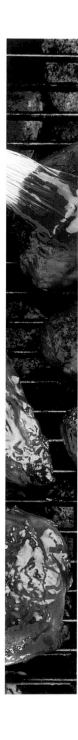

Southwestern Chicken Salad

1 package (1.27 ounces) LAWRY'S® Spices & Seasonings for Fajitas
3 tablespoons vegetable oil
2½ tablespoons lime juice
1½ teaspoons LAWRY'S® Garlic Powder With Parsley
6 boneless, skinless chicken breasts (about 1½ pounds)
6 cups torn lettuce
½ red onion, thinly sliced
1 large tomato, cut into wedges
1 avocado, thinly sliced
Ranch-style dressing

In small bowl, mix together Spices & Seasonings for Fajitas, oil, lime juice and Garlic Powder With Parsley. Rinse and pierce chicken with fork several times. Place chicken in large Ziploc® bag. Pour on fajitas-marinade mixture; seal bag and toss to coat chicken. Refrigerate for 30 minutes to overnight. Remove chicken from bag; discarding marinade. Grill or broil until chicken is no longer pink and juices run clear when cut, about 10 to 15 minutes. Let cool slightly, slice thinly or cut into cubes. To arrange salads, place chicken on beds of lettuce. Top each with equal portions of onion, tomato and avocado. Drizzle with ranch-style dressing.

Makes 4 to 6 servings

Prep Time: 15 minutes
Marinate Time: 30 minutes
Cook Time: 10 to 15 minutes

Southwestern Chicken Salad

Spicy Mango Chicken

¼ cup mango nectar
¼ cup chopped fresh cilantro
2 jalapeño chile peppers, seeded and finely chopped
2 teaspoons vegetable oil
2 teaspoons LAWRY'S® Seasoned Salt
½ teaspoon LAWRY'S® Garlic Powder with Parsley
½ teaspoon ground cumin
4 boneless, skinless chicken breasts (about 1 pound)
Mango & Black Bean Salsa (recipe follows)

In small bowl, combine all ingredients except chicken and salsa; mix well. Brush marinade on both sides of chicken. Grill or broil chicken 10 to 15 minutes or until no longer pink in center and juices run clear when cut, turning once and basting often with additional marinade. *Do not baste during last 5 minutes of cooking.* Discard any remaining marinade. Top chicken with Mango & Black Bean Salsa.

Makes 4 servings

Hint: Jalapeño peppers can sting and irritate the skin; wear rubber gloves when handling peppers and do not touch eyes.

Mango & Black Bean Salsa

1 ripe mango, peeled, seeded and chopped
1 cup canned black beans, rinsed and drained
½ cup chopped tomato
2 thinly sliced green onions
1 tablespoon chopped fresh cilantro
1½ teaspoons lime juice
1½ teaspoons red wine vinegar
½ teaspoon LAWRY'S® Seasoned Salt

In medium bowl, combine all ingredients; mix well. Let stand 30 minutes to allow flavors to blend.

Makes about 2¾ cups

Serving Suggestion: Serve with chicken or fish.

Spicy Mango Chicken

Chicken Teriyaki Kabobs

1 cup LAWRY'S® Teriyaki Marinade With Pineapple Juice, divided
1 pound boneless, skinless chicken breasts, cut in 1-inch cubes
½ teaspoon LAWRY'S® Seasoned Pepper
½ teaspoon LAWRY'S® Garlic Powder With Parsley
2 medium zucchini, cut in ½-inch slices
1 medium green bell pepper, cut in 1-inch squares
1 small red onion, cut in ½-inch chunks
Skewers

In large resealable plastic bag, combine ¾ cup Teriyaki Marinade and chicken. Marinate in refrigerator 30 minutes. Remove chicken from bag and discard used marinade. Sprinkle chicken with Seasoned Pepper and Garlic Powder With Parsley. Thread chicken onto skewers alternating with remaining ingredients. Grill until thoroughly cooked, about 10 minutes on each side, brushing with remaining ¼ cup Marinade. *Makes 6 servings*

Meal Idea: Wonderful for picnics and grill parties. For wrap sandwiches, remove skewers after grilling and serve in flour tortillas.

Prep Time: 10 minutes
Marinate Time: 30 minutes
Cook Time: 10 to 12 minutes

Kabobs were probably invented centuries ago when hungry Turkish horsemen would light large fires and skewer pieces of meat on their swords to cook.

Chicken Teriyaki Kabobs

Lime-Mustard Marinated Chicken

2 boneless skinless chicken breasts (about 3 ounces each)
¼ cup fresh lime juice
3 tablespoons honey mustard, divided
2 teaspoons olive oil
¼ teaspoon ground cumin
⅛ teaspoon garlic powder
⅛ teaspoon ground red pepper
¾ cup plus 2 tablespoons chicken broth, divided
¼ cup uncooked rice
1 cup broccoli florets
⅓ cup matchstick-size carrot pieces

1. Rinse chicken. Pat dry with paper towels. Place in resealable plastic food storage bag. Whisk together lime juice, 2 tablespoons mustard, olive oil, cumin, garlic powder and red pepper. Pour over chicken. Seal bag. Marinate in refrigerator 2 hours.

2. Combine ¾ cup chicken broth, rice and remaining 1 tablespoon mustard in small saucepan. Bring to a boil. Reduce heat and simmer, covered, 12 minutes or until rice is almost tender. Stir in broccoli, carrots and remaining 2 tablespoons chicken broth. Cook, covered, 2 to 3 minutes more or until vegetables are crisp-tender and rice is tender.

3. Meanwhile, drain chicken, discard marinade. Prepare grill for direct grilling. Grill chicken over medium coals 10 to 13 minutes or until no longer pink in center. Serve chicken with rice mixture. *Makes 2 servings*

Lime-Mustard Marinated Chicken

Grilled Marinated Chicken

8 whole chicken legs (about 3½ pounds)
6 ounces frozen lemonade concentrate, thawed
2 tablespoons white wine vinegar
1 tablespoon grated lemon peel
2 cloves garlic, minced

1. Remove skin and all visible fat from chicken. Place chicken in 13×9-inch glass baking dish. Combine remaining ingredients in small bowl; blend well. Pour over chicken; turn to coat. Cover; refrigerate 3 hours or overnight, turning occasionally.

2. To prevent sticking, spray grid with nonstick cooking spray. Prepare coals for grilling.

3. Place chicken on grill 4 inches from medium-hot coals. Grill 20 to 30 minutes or until chicken is no longer pink near bone, turning occasionally. Garnish with curly endive and lemon peel strips, if desired. *Makes 8 servings*

Grilled Turkey

Sage-Garlic Baste (page 130)
1 whole turkey (9 to 13 pounds), thawed if frozen
Salt and black pepper
3 lemons, halved (optional)

Prepare Sage-Garlic Baste. Remove neck and giblets from turkey. Rinse turkey under cold running water; pat dry with paper towels. Season turkey cavity with salt and pepper; place lemons in cavity, if desired. Lightly brush outer surface of turkey with part of Sage-Garlic Baste. Pull skin over neck and secure with skewer. Tuck wing tips under back and tie legs together with cotton string. Insert heatproof meat thermometer into thickest part of thigh, not touching bone. Arrange medium-hot KINGSFORD® Briquets on each side of large rectangular metal or foil drip pan. Pour hot tap water into drip pan until half full. Place turkey, breast side up, on grid directly above drip pan. Grill turkey on covered grill 9 to 13 minutes per pound or until thermometer registers 180°F, basting every 20 minutes with remaining Sage-Garlic Baste. Add a few briquets to both sides of fire every hour or as necessary to maintain constant temperature.* Let turkey stand 15 minutes before carving. Refrigerate leftovers promptly. *Makes 8 to 10 servings*

*For larger turkey, add 15 briquets every 50 to 60 minutes.

continued on page 130

Grilled Marinated Chicken

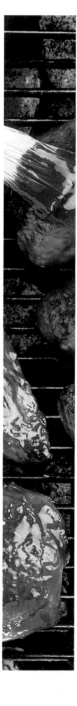

Grilled Turkey, *continued*

Sage-Garlic Baste

> **Grated peel and juice of 1 lemon**
> **3 tablespoons olive oil**
> **2 tablespoons minced fresh sage** *or* **1½ teaspoons rubbed sage**
> **2 cloves garlic, minced**
> **½ teaspoon salt**
> **¼ teaspoon black pepper**

Combine all ingredients in small saucepan; cook and stir over medium heat 4 minutes. Use as baste for turkey or chicken. *Makes about ½ cup*

Asian Turkey Burgers

> **1 pound ground turkey**
> **1⅓ cups *French's*® French Fried Onions, divided**
> **1 egg**
> **½ cup finely chopped water chestnuts**
> **¼ cup dry bread crumbs**
> **3 tablespoons Oriental stir-fry sauce or teriyaki baste & glaze sauce**
> **1 tablespoon *Frank's*® *RedHot*® Original Cayenne Pepper Sauce**
> **2 teaspoons grated fresh ginger** *or* **½ teaspoon ground ginger**
> **4 sandwich buns**
> **Shredded lettuce**

Combine turkey, *1 cup* French Fried Onions, egg, water chestnuts, bread crumbs, stir-fry sauce, **Frank's RedHot** Sauce and ginger in large bowl. Shape into 4 patties.

Grill patties over medium coals 10 minutes or until no longer pink in center, turning once, or broil patties 6 inches from heat. Serve on buns. Top with remaining ⅓ cup onions and lettuce. *Makes 4 servings*

Prep Time: 15 minutes
Cook Time: 10 minutes

Asian Turkey Burger

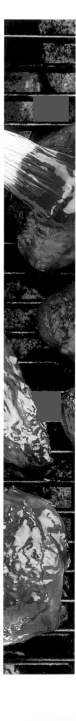

Grilled Garlic Chicken

1 envelope LIPTON® RECIPE SECRETS® Savory Herb with Garlic Soup Mix
3 tablespoons BERTOLLI® Olive Oil
4 boneless, skinless chicken breast halves (about 1¼ pounds)

1. In medium bowl, combine soup mix with oil.

2. Add chicken; toss to coat.

3. Grill or broil until chicken is thoroughly cooked.   *Makes 4 servings*

BBQ Turkey with Pineapple Relish

2 pounds boneless skinless turkey breast roast

Marinade
Grated peel and juice from 1 orange
2 tablespoons red wine vinegar
4½ teaspoons dried oregano leaves, crushed
1 tablespoon packed brown sugar
2 teaspoons vegetable oil
5 cloves garlic, pressed
Salt and pepper to taste

Pineapple Relish
1 DOLE® Fresh Pineapple
1 medium tomato, seeded and chopped
1 small red onion, minced
½ cup DOLE® Pitted Prunes, snipped
¼ cup chopped cilantro
2 tablespoons lime juice
1 tablespoon white vinegar
1 tablespoon drained capers

• Cut 4 (1-inch) slashes in both sides of turkey. Place in glass casserole dish.

• Combine marinade ingredients in small bowl. Pour over turkey. Cover; marinate in refrigerator 30 minutes or overnight, turning occasionally.

continued on page 134

Grilled Garlic Chicken

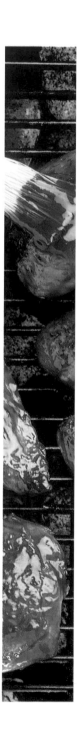

BBQ Turkey with Pineapple Relish, *continued*

- Twist crown from pineapple. Cut pineapple in half lengthwise. Cut fruit from shells with knife. Trim off core. Cut half of fruit crosswise into thin slices for garnish; reserve. Coarsely chop remaining fruit; combine with remaining relish ingredients in medium bowl.

- Drain turkey; boil marinade one minute. Place turkey 6 inches above medium hot coals. Grill, uncovered, turning and basting every 5 minutes with marinade 30 to 35 minutes or until meat thermometer registers 170°F. Let stand 5 minutes. Slice; serve with Pineapple Relish. Garnish with reserved pineapple slices.   *Makes 6 servings*

Lemon Chicken and Vegetables

8 ounces uncooked spaghetti
1 pound boneless skinless chicken breasts
1 large green bell pepper, cut in half
1 large red bell pepper, cut in half
1 medium yellow summer squash, cut in half lengthwise
½ cup finely chopped fresh parsley
⅓ cup dry white wine
2 tablespoons fresh lemon juice
2 tablespoons olive oil
3 cloves garlic, minced
2 teaspoons finely grated lemon peel
¼ teaspoon salt
¼ teaspoon black pepper

1. Cook pasta according to package directions, omitting salt. Drain; set aside.

2. Spray grid with nonstick cooking spray. Prepare coals for grilling. Place chicken, peppers and squash on grill 5 to 6 inches from medium-hot coals. Grill 10 to 12 minutes or until chicken is no longer pink in center and vegetables are soft to the touch. Remove from grill. Cool slightly; cut into ½-inch pieces.

3. Combine parsley, wine, lemon juice, oil, garlic, lemon peel, salt and pepper in medium bowl. Toss cooked chicken and vegetables with ⅓ cup sauce. Toss pasta with remaining sauce. Place chicken and vegetables over pasta; serve.

Makes 8 servings

Prep Time: 15 minutes
Cook Time: 15 minutes

Lemon Chicken and Vegetables

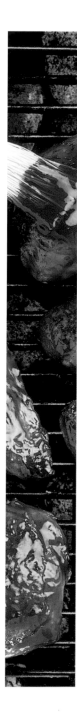

Honey and Mustard Glazed Chicken

1 whole chicken (4 to 5 pounds)
1 tablespoon vegetable oil
¼ cup honey
2 tablespoons Dijon mustard
1 tablespoon reduced-sodium soy sauce
½ teaspoon ground ginger
⅛ teaspoon black pepper
Dash salt

1. Prepare grill for indirect cooking.

2. Remove giblets from chicken cavity; reserve for another use or discard. Rinse chicken with cold water; pat dry with paper towels. Pull skin over neck; secure with metal skewer. Tuck wings under back; tie legs together with wet string. Lightly brush chicken with oil.

3. Combine honey, mustard, soy sauce, ginger, pepper and salt in small bowl; set aside.

4. Place chicken, breast side up, on grid directly over drip pan. Grill, covered, over medium-high heat 1 hour 30 minutes or until internal temperature reaches 180°F when tested with meat thermometer inserted into thickest part of thigh, not touching bone. Brush with honey mixture every 10 minutes during last 30 minutes of cooking time.*

5. Transfer chicken to cutting board; cover with foil. Let stand 15 minutes before carving. Internal temperature will continue to rise 5°F to 10°F during stand time.

Makes 4 to 5 servings

*If using grill with heat on one side (rather than around drip pan), rotate chicken 180° after 45 minutes of cooking time.

Honey and Mustard Glazed Chicken

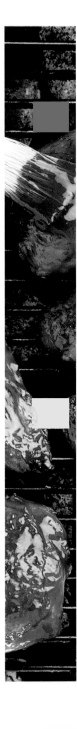

Chicken Roll-Ups

¼ **cup fresh lemon juice**
1 **tablespoon olive oil**
¼ **teaspoon salt**
¼ **teaspoon black pepper**
4 **boneless skinless chicken breasts**
¼ **cup finely chopped fresh Italian parsley**
2 **tablespoons grated Parmesan cheese**
2 **tablespoons chopped fresh chives**
1 **teaspoon finely grated lemon peel**
2 **large cloves garlic, minced**
16 **toothpicks soaked in hot water 15 minutes**

1. Combine lemon juice, oil, salt and pepper in 11×7-inch casserole. Pound chicken to ⅜-inch thickness. Place chicken in lemon mixture; turn to coat. Cover; marinate in refrigerator at least 30 minutes.

2. Prepare grill for direct cooking.

3. Combine parsley, cheese, chives, lemon peel and garlic in small bowl. Discard chicken marinade. Spread ¼ of parsley mixture over each chicken breast, leaving an inch around edges free. Starting at narrow end, roll chicken to enclose filling; secure with toothpicks.

4. Grill chicken, covered, over medium-hot coals about 2 minutes on each side or until golden brown. Transfer chicken to low heat; grill, covered, about 5 minutes or until chicken is no longer pink in center.

5. Remove toothpicks; slice each chicken breast into 5 or 6 pieces.

Makes 4 servings

Chicken Roll-Up

Grilled Chicken and Fresh Salsa Wraps

1¼ cups LAWRY'S® Herb & Garlic Marinade With Lemon Juice, divided
4 boneless, skinless chicken breasts (about 1 pound)
1 large tomato, chopped
1 can (4 ounces) diced green chiles, drained (optional)
¼ cup thinly sliced green onions
1 tablespoon red wine vinegar
1 tablespoon chopped fresh cilantro
½ teaspoon LAWRY'S® Garlic Salt
4 burrito size *or* 8 fajita size flour tortillas, warmed to soften

In large resealable plastic bag, combine 1 cup Herb & Garlic Marinade and chicken; seal bag and marinate in refrigerator at least 30 minutes. In medium bowl, combine tomato, chiles, onions, remaining ¼ cup Herb & Garlic Marinade, vinegar, cilantro and Garlic Salt; mix well. Cover salsa and refrigerate 30 minutes or until chilled. Remove chicken from bag, discarding used marinade. Grill or broil chicken about 10 to 15 minutes, or until thoroughly cooked, turning halfway through grilling time. Slice chicken into strips. Place chicken on tortillas; spoon salsa mixture on top and wrap to enclose. Serve immediately.   *Makes 4 servings*

Meal Idea: This is an excellent recipe for picnics and outdoor dining. Wrap each filled tortilla with plastic wrap and keep chilled until ready to serve. You may also choose to assemble wraps when ready to serve outdoors!

Prep Time: 12 to 15 minutes
Marinate Time: 30 minutes
Cook Time: 10 to 15 minutes

Grilled Chicken and Fresh Salsa Wrap

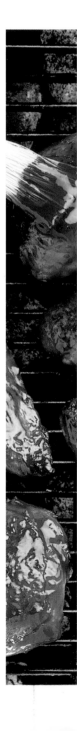

Grilled Chicken and Melon Salad

¾ **cup orange marmalade, divided**
¼ **cup plus 2 tablespoons white wine vinegar, divided**
2 **tablespoons reduced-sodium soy sauce**
1 **tablespoon grated fresh ginger**
½ **cantaloupe, cut into 1-inch-thick slices**
½ **honeydew melon, cut into 1-inch-thick slices**
4 **boneless skinless chicken breasts**
2 **tablespoons olive oil**
2 **tablespoons minced fresh cilantro**
1 **teaspoon jalapeño pepper sauce**
10 **cups mixed lettuce greens**
1 **pint fresh strawberries, halved**

1. Combine ⅓ cup orange marmalade, 2 tablespoons vinegar, soy sauce and ginger. Brush marmalade mixture over melons, then over chicken. Arrange melons in grill basket or thread onto skewers.

2. Grill chicken over hot coals 5 to 7 minutes on each side or until no longer pink in center. Grill melons, covered, 2 to 3 minutes on each side. Refrigerate overnight.

3. Combine remaining marmalade, ¼ cup vinegar, oil, cilantro and jalapeño pepper sauce in jar with tight-fitting lid; shake well to blend.

4. To complete recipe, arrange lettuce, chicken, melon and strawberries on serving plates; spoon marmalade mixture over top.   *Makes 4 servings*

Tip: For a special touch, garnish with fresh produce such as red and green bell peppers or jalapeño peppers.

Make-Ahead Time: up to 1 day before serving
Final Prep Time: 5 minutes

Grilled Chicken and Melon Salad

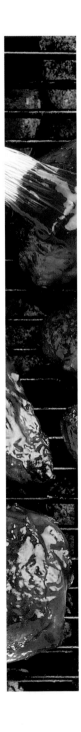

Rotisserie Chicken with Pesto Brush

2 BUTTERBALL® Fresh Young Roasters
½ cup olive oil
½ cup balsamic vinegar
¼ cup chopped fresh oregano
¼ cup chopped fresh parsley
2 tablespoons chopped fresh rosemary
2 tablespoons chopped fresh thyme

Combine oil, vinegar, oregano, parsley, rosemary and thyme in small bowl. Roast chicken according to rotisserie directions. Dip brush into herb mixture; brush chicken with herb mixture every 30 minutes for first 2 hours of roasting. Brush every 15 minutes during last hour of roasting. Roast chicken until internal temperature reaches 180°F in thigh and meat is no longer pink.   *Makes 16 servings*

Tip: To make an aromatic herb brush, bundle sprigs of rosemary, thyme, oregano and parsley together. Tie bundle with kitchen string. Use as brush for pesto.

Prep Time: 15 minutes plus roasting time

Rotisserie Chicken with Pesto Brush

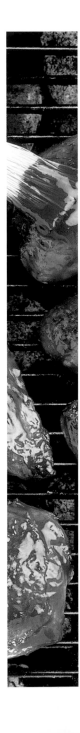

Grilled Ginger Chicken with Pineapple and Coconut Rice

1 can (20 ounces) pineapple rings in juice
⅔ cup uncooked white rice
½ cup unsweetened flaked coconut
4 boneless skinless chicken breasts (about 1 pound)
1 tablespoon soy sauce
1 teaspoon ground ginger

1. Drain juice from pineapple into glass measure. Reserve 2 tablespoons juice. Combine remaining juice with enough water to equal 2 cups.

2. Cook and stir rice and coconut in medium saucepan over medium heat 3 to 4 minutes or until lightly browned. Add juice mixture; cover and bring to a boil. Reduce heat to low; cook 15 minutes or until rice is tender and liquid is absorbed.

3. While rice is cooking, combine chicken, reserved juice, soy sauce and ginger in medium bowl; toss well.

4. Grill chicken 6 minutes; turn. Add pineapple to grill. Cook 6 to 8 minutes or until chicken is no longer pink in center, turning pineapple after 3 minutes.

5. Transfer rice to four serving plates; serve with chicken and pineapple.

Makes 4 servings

Prep and Cook Time: 22 minutes

More than 76% of American households
own a grill.

Grilled Ginger Chicken with Pineapple and Coconut Rice

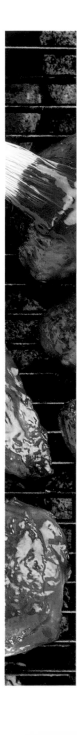

Grilled Chicken Breasts with Zesty Peanut Sauce

8 large boneless, skinless chicken breast halves

Marinade
½ **cup soy sauce**
⅓ **cup fresh lime juice**
¼ **cup CRISCO® All-Vegetable Oil**
2 **tablespoons JIF® Creamy or Extra Crunchy Peanut Butter**
1 **tablespoon brown sugar**
2 **large cloves garlic, minced**
½ **teaspoon salt**
½ **teaspoon cayenne pepper**

Sauce
1 **cup JIF® Creamy or Extra Crunchy Peanut Butter**
1 **cup unsweetened coconut milk**
¼ **cup fresh lime juice**
3 **tablespoons soy sauce**
2 **tablespoons dark brown sugar**
2 **teaspoons minced fresh ginger root**
2 **cloves garlic, minced**
¼ **teaspoon cayenne pepper, or to taste**
½ **cup chicken stock**
½ **cup heavy cream**
   Chopped fresh cilantro for garnish

Wash, trim and pound the chicken to ¼-inch thickness.

Combine chicken and marinade ingredients in a plastic bag. Marinate 1 hour or overnight in the refrigerator.

Combine sauce ingredients in a saucepan over medium heat. Cook 15 minutes, stirring constantly. Whisk in stock and cream. Cook 1 minute. Set aside.

Preheat grill. Remove chicken from marinade and place on hot grid. Grill 4 to 6 minutes on each side or until center is no longer pink. Serve hot topped with the peanut sauce. Sprinkle with cilantro.   *Makes 8 servings*

Grilled Chicken Breasts with Zesty Peanut Sauce

The International Grill

Thai Satay Chicken Skewers

    1 pound boneless skinless chicken breasts
    ⅓ cup soy sauce
    2 tablespoons fresh lime juice
    2 cloves garlic, minced
    1 teaspoon grated fresh ginger
    ¾ teaspoon red pepper flakes
    2 tablespoons water
    ¾ cup canned unsweetened coconut milk
    1 tablespoon creamy peanut butter
    4 green onions with tops, cut into 1-inch pieces

1. Cut chicken crosswise into ⅜-inch-wide strips; place in shallow glass dish.

2. Combine soy sauce, lime juice, garlic, ginger and red pepper flakes in small bowl. Reserve 3 tablespoons mixture; cover and refrigerate. Add water to remaining mixture. Pour over chicken; toss to coat well. Cover; marinate in refrigerator at least 30 minutes or up to 2 hours, stirring mixture occasionally.

3. Soak 8 (10- to 12-inch) bamboo skewers 20 minutes in cold water to prevent them from burning; drain. Prepare grill for direct cooking.

4. Meanwhile, for peanut sauce, combine coconut milk, 3 tablespoons reserved soy sauce mixture and peanut butter in small saucepan. Bring to a boil over medium-high heat, stirring constantly. Reduce heat and simmer, uncovered, 2 to 4 minutes or until sauce thickens. Keep warm.

5. Drain chicken; reserve marinade. Weave 3 to 4 chicken strips accordion-style onto each skewer, alternating with green onion pieces. Brush chicken and onions with reserved marinade. Discard remaining marinade.

6. Place skewers on grid. Grill skewers on uncovered grill over medium-hot coals 6 to 8 minutes or until chicken is no longer pink, turning halfway through grilling time. Serve with warm peanut sauce for dipping.   *Makes 4 servings*

Thai Satay Chicken Skewers

Teriyaki Salmon with Asian Slaw

4 tablespoons reduced-sodium teriyaki sauce, divided
2 (5- to 6-ounce) boneless salmon fillets with skin (1 inch thick)
2½ cups packaged coleslaw mix
1 cup fresh or frozen snow peas, cut lengthwise into thin strips
½ cup thinly sliced radishes
2 tablespoons orange marmalade
1 teaspoon dark sesame oil

1. Prepare grill for direct cooking. Spoon 2 tablespoons teriyaki sauce over meaty sides of salmon. Let stand while preparing vegetable mixture.

2. Combine coleslaw mix, snow peas and radishes in large bowl. Combine remaining 2 tablespoons teriyaki sauce, marmalade and sesame oil in small bowl. Add to coleslaw mixture; toss well.

3. Grill salmon, flesh side down, over medium coals without turning 6 to 10 minutes until center is opaque.

4. Transfer coleslaw mixture to serving plates; top with salmon.

Makes 2 servings

The word barbecue is also written BBQ, barbeque, and sometimes abbreviated as Q or Cue.

Teriyaki Salmon with Asian Slaw

Javanese Pork Saté

1 pound boneless pork loin
½ cup minced onion
2 tablespoons peanut butter
2 tablespoons lemon juice
2 tablespoons soy sauce
1 tablespoon brown sugar
1 tablespoon vegetable oil
1 clove garlic, minced
Dash hot pepper sauce

Cut pork into ½-inch cubes; place in shallow dish. In blender or food processor combine remaining ingredients. Blend until smooth. Pour over pork. Cover and marinate in refrigerator 10 minutes. Thread pork onto skewers. (If using bamboo skewers, soak in water 1 hour to prevent burning.)

Grill or broil 10 to 12 minutes, turning occasionally, until done. Serve with hot cooked rice, if desired.   *Makes 4 servings*

Favorite recipe from **National Pork Board**

Fajitas on a Stick

1 pound boneless, skinless chicken breasts, cut into 1-inch pieces
½ green bell pepper, cut into ½-inch pieces
½ onion, sliced into ½-inch slices
16 cherry tomatoes
8 wooden skewers, soaked in water for 30 minutes
1 cup LAWRY'S® Tequila Lime Marinade With Lime Juice
8 fajita size flour tortillas, warmed to soften

Thread chicken, pepper, onion and tomatoes onto skewers, dividing up ingredients equally. Brush heavily and frequently with Tequila Lime Marinade while grilling. Cook chicken 18 minutes or until thoroughly cooked. Place cooked skewer on warm tortilla; remove fajitas from skewer and roll-up tortilla to enclose fajita mixture securely. Serve immediately.   *Makes 8 fajitas*

Prep Time: 20 minutes
Cook Time: 15 to 18 minutes

Javanese Pork Saté

Carne Asada

1½ pounds top sirloin steak
¼ cup lemon juice
2 tablespoons vegetable oil
1 tablespoon chopped cilantro, optional
2 teaspoons LAWRY'S® Garlic Salt
1 teaspoon LAWRY'S® Seasoned Pepper
1 teaspoon LAWRY'S® Seasoned Salt

Place steak in large resealable plastic bag. Add remaining ingredients and shake to mix; marinate in refrigerator for 30 minutes to overnight. Remove steak from bag, discarding used marinade mixture. Grill or broil steak until cooked to desired doneness, about 5 minutes on each side. Shake on additional Garlic Salt during cooking for extra flavor. *Makes 4 servings*

Prep Time: 5 minutes

Moroccan Swordfish

4 swordfish steaks (4 ounces each), about 1 inch thick
1 tablespoon fresh lemon juice
1 tablespoon apple cider vinegar
2½ teaspoons garlic-flavored vegetable oil
1 teaspoon *each* ground ginger and paprika
½ teaspoon ground cumin
½ teaspoon hot chili oil
¼ teaspoon *each* salt and ground coriander
⅛ teaspoon black pepper
2⅔ cups prepared couscous

1. Place swordfish in single layer in medium shallow dish. Combine lemon juice, vinegar, garlic-flavored oil, ginger, paprika, cumin, chili oil, salt, coriander and pepper in small bowl; pour over swordfish and turn to coat both sides. Cover and refrigerate 40 minutes, turning once.

2. Discard marinade; grill swordfish on uncovered grill over medium-hot coals 8 to 10 minutes or until swordfish is opaque, turning once. Serve with couscous. *Makes 4 servings*

Carne Asada

Middle Eastern Grilled Vegetable Wraps

1 large eggplant (about 1 pound), cut crosswise into ⅜-inch slices
 Nonstick cooking spray
¾ pound large fresh mushrooms
1 medium red bell pepper, seeded, cored and quartered
1 medium green bell pepper, seeded, cored and quartered
2 green onions, sliced
¼ cup fresh lemon juice
⅛ teaspoon black pepper
4 large (10-inch) flour tortillas
½ cup (4 ounces) hummus (chick-pea spread)*
⅓ cup lightly packed fresh cilantro
12 large fresh basil leaves
12 large fresh mint leaves

*Four ounces crumbled reduced-fat feta cheese can be substituted for hummus.

1. Prepare barbecue grill for direct cooking.

2. Lightly spray eggplant with cooking spray. If mushrooms are small, thread onto skewers.

3. Grill bell peppers, skin-side down, over hot coals until skins are blackened. Place in paper bag; seal. Steam 5 minutes; remove skin. Grill eggplant and mushrooms, covered, over medium coals about 2 minutes on each side or until tender and lightly browned. Cut eggplant and peppers into ½-inch strips; cut mushrooms into quarters. Combine vegetables, onions, lemon juice and black pepper in medium bowl.

4. Grill tortillas on both sides about 1 minute or until warmed. Spoon ¼ of hummus, ¼ of herbs, and ¼ of vegetables down center of each tortilla. Roll to enclose filling; serve immediately. *Makes 4 servings*

Middle Eastern Grilled Vegetable Wrap

Jamaican Baby Back Ribs

2 tablespoons sugar
2 tablespoons fresh lemon juice
1 tablespoon salt
1 tablespoon vegetable oil
2 teaspoons black pepper
2 teaspoons dried thyme leaves
¾ teaspoon *each* ground cinnamon, nutmeg and allspice
½ teaspoon ground red pepper
6 pounds well-trimmed pork baby back ribs, cut into 3- to 4-rib
   portions
Barbecue Sauce (recipe follows)

1. For seasoning rub, combine all ingredients except ribs and Barbecue Sauce in small bowl; stir well. Spread over all surfaces of ribs; press with fingertips so mixture adheres to ribs. Cover; refrigerate overnight.

2. Prepare grill for indirect cooking. While coals are heating, prepare Barbecue Sauce.

3. Place seasoned ribs on grid directly over drip pan. Grill, covered, 1 hour, turning occasionally. Baste ribs generously with Barbecue Sauce; grill 30 minutes more or until ribs are tender and browned, turning occasionally.

4. Bring remaining Barbecue Sauce to a boil over medium-high heat; boil 1 minute. Serve ribs with remaining sauce. *Makes 6 servings*

Barbecue Sauce

2 tablespoons butter
½ cup finely chopped onion
1½ cups ketchup
1 cup red currant jelly
¼ cup apple cider vinegar
1 tablespoon soy sauce
¼ teaspoon each ground red and black peppers

Melt butter in medium saucepan over medium-high heat. Add onion; cook and stir until softened. Stir in remaining ingredients. Reduce heat to medium-low; simmer 20 minutes, stirring often. *Makes about 3 cups*

Jamaican Baby Back Ribs

Italian Mixed Seafood

½ pound large raw shrimp, peeled and deveined
½ pound sea scallops
1 small zucchini, cut into ½-inch pieces
1 small red bell pepper, cut into ½-inch pieces
1 small red onion, cut into wedges
12 large mushrooms
1 bottle (8 ounces) Italian salad dressing
2 teaspoons dried Italian seasoning, divided
1½ cups uncooked brown rice
2 cans (about 14 ounces each) chicken broth

1. Place shrimp, scallops, zucchini, bell pepper, onion, mushrooms, salad dressing and 1 teaspoon Italian seasoning in large resealable plastic food storage bag. Close bag securely, turning to coat. Marinate in refrigerator 30 minutes, turning after 15 minutes.

2. Meanwhile, place rice, chicken broth and remaining 1 teaspoon Italian seasoning in medium saucepan over high heat. Bring to a boil; cover and reduce heat to low. Simmer 35 minutes or until liquid is absorbed.

3. Meanwhile, prepare grill for direct cooking.

4. Drain seafood and vegetables; reserve marinade. Place seafood and vegetables in lightly oiled grill basket or on vegetable grilling grid. Grill, covered, over medium-high heat 4 to 5 minutes; turn and baste with marinade. Grill 4 to 5 minutes or until shrimp are opaque. Serve seafood and vegetables over rice.

Makes 4 to 6 servings

Italian Mixed Seafood

Cuban Garlic & Lime Pork Chops

6 boneless pork top loin chops, ¾ inch thick (about 1½ pounds)
2 tablespoons olive oil
2 tablespoons lime juice
2 tablespoons orange juice
2 teaspoons bottled minced garlic
½ teaspoon salt, divided
½ teaspoon red pepper flakes
2 small seedless oranges, peeled and chopped
1 medium cucumber, peeled, seeded and chopped
2 tablespoons chopped onion
2 tablespoons chopped fresh cilantro

1. Place pork in large resealable plastic food storage bag. Add oil, juices, garlic, ¼ teaspoon salt and pepper flakes. Seal bag and shake to evenly distribute marinade; refrigerate up to 24 hours.

2. To make salsa, combine oranges, cucumber, onion and cilantro in small bowl; toss lightly. Cover and refrigerate 1 hour or overnight. Add remaining ¼ teaspoon salt just before serving.

3. To complete recipe, remove pork from marinade; discard marinade. Grill pork 6 to 8 minutes on each side or until pork is no longer pink in center. Serve with salsa.

Makes 4 servings

Make-Ahead Time: 1 day before cooking
Final Prep and Cook Time: 16 minutes

Cuban Garlic & Lime Pork Chop

Grilled Summer Gazpacho

1 red bell pepper, stemmed, seeded and halved
4 large (about 2 pounds) tomatoes, tops removed
1 small onion, halved
   Nonstick cooking spray
4 cloves garlic, divided
6 (½-inch) slices French bread
1 cup coarsely chopped peeled cucumber
1 cup day-old French bread cubes, soaked in water and squeezed dry
2 to 4 tablespoons chopped fresh cilantro
2 tablespoons lemon juice
1 tablespoon olive oil
½ teaspoon salt
2 cups ice water
   Additional cilantro leaves for garnish

1. Prepare coals for direct grilling. Grill bell pepper halves, skin sides down, on covered grill over medium-hot coals 15 to 25 minutes or until skin is charred, without turning. Remove from grill and place in plastic bag until cool enough to handle, about 10 minutes. Remove skin; set peppers aside to cool.

2. Meanwhile, spray tomatoes and onion halves with cooking spray. Grill tomatoes and onion halves, skin sides down, on covered grill over medium coals 10 to 20 minutes or until grillmarked and tender, turning as needed. Thread 3 garlic cloves onto water-soaked wooden skewer. Spray with cooking spray. Grill garlic on covered grill over medium coals about 8 minutes or until browned and tender. Remove vegetables from grill and let cool on cutting board.

3. While vegetables cool, cut remaining garlic clove in half. Spray both sides of French bread slices with cooking spray; rub with garlic clove halves. Grill bread slices on both sides until toasted and golden, watching carefully. Cool; cut into ½-inch croutons and set aside for garnish.

4. Gently squeeze cooled tomatoes to remove seeds and release skins. Scrape and discard any excess charring from onion. Coarsely chop bell pepper, tomatoes and onion; add with cucumber to food processor or blender. Cover and process until smooth. Transfer to large bowl.

5. Add soaked bread cubes, chopped cilantro, lemon juice, oil and salt to food processor; cover and process until smooth. Combine with grilled vegetable mixture; stir in ice water. Ladle soup into bowls; garnish with garlic croutons and additional cilantro leaves, if desired.
Makes 6 servings

Grilled Summer Gazpacho

Greek Lamb Burgers

¼ **cup pine nuts**
1 **pound lean ground lamb**
¼ **cup finely chopped yellow onion**
3 **cloves garlic, minced, divided**
¾ **teaspoon salt**
¼ **teaspoon black pepper**
¼ **cup plain yogurt**
¼ **teaspoon sugar**
4 **slices red onion (¼ inch thick)**
1 **tablespoon olive oil**
8 **pumpernickel bread slices**
12 **thin cucumber slices**
4 **tomato slices**

1. Prepare grill for direct cooking. Meanwhile, heat small skillet over medium heat until hot. Add pine nuts; cook 30 to 45 seconds until light brown, shaking pan occasionally.

2. Combine lamb, pine nuts, yellow onion, 2 cloves garlic, salt and pepper in large bowl; mix well. Shape mixture into 4 patties, about ½ inch thick and 4 inches in diameter. Combine yogurt, sugar and remaining 1 clove garlic in small bowl; set aside.

3. Brush 1 side of each patty and red onion slice with oil; place on grid, oiled sides down. Brush tops with oil. Grill, on covered grill, over medium-hot coals 8 to 10 minutes or until internal temperature reaches 160°F, turning halfway through grilling time. Place bread on grid to toast during last few minutes of grilling time; grill 1 to 2 minutes per side.

4. Top 4 bread slices with patties and red onion slices; top each with 3 cucumber slices and 1 tomato slice. Dollop evenly with yogurt mixture. Top sandwiches with remaining 4 bread slices. Serve immediately. *Makes 4 servings*

Greek Lamb Burger

Chicken Tikka
(Tandoori-Style Grilled Chicken)

2 chickens (3 pounds each), cut up
1 pint nonfat yogurt
½ cup *Frank's® RedHot®* Original Cayenne Pepper Sauce
1 tablespoon grated peeled fresh ginger
3 cloves garlic, minced
1 tablespoon paprika
1 tablespoon cumin seeds, crushed *or* 1½ teaspoons ground cumin
2 teaspoons salt
1 teaspoon ground coriander

Remove skin and visible fat from chicken pieces. Rinse with cold water and pat dry. Randomly poke chicken all over with tip of sharp knife. Place chicken in resealable plastic food storage bags or large glass bowl. Combine yogurt, **Frank's RedHot** Sauce, ginger, garlic, paprika, cumin, salt and coriander in small bowl; mix well. Pour over chicken pieces, turning pieces to coat evenly. Seal bags or cover bowl and marinate in refrigerator 1 hour or overnight.

Place chicken on oiled grid, reserving marinade. Grill over medium coals 45 minutes or until chicken is no longer pink near bone and juices run clear, turning and basting often with marinade. (Do not baste during last 10 minutes of cooking.) Discard any remaining marinade. Serve warm. *Makes 6 to 8 servings*

Prep Time: 15 minutes
Marinate Time: 1 hour
Cook Time: 45 minutes

Chicken Tikka (Tandoori-Style Grilled Chicken)

Serbian Lamb Sausage Kabobs

1 pound lean ground lamb
1 pound 90% lean ground beef
1 small onion, finely chopped
2 cloves garlic, minced
1 tablespoon hot Hungarian paprika
1 small egg, lightly beaten
  Salt and black pepper to taste
3 to 4 red, green or yellow bell peppers, cut into squares
  Rice pilaf for serving
  Tomato slices and green onion brushes for garnish

1. Combine lamb, beef, finely chopped onion, garlic, paprika and egg in large bowl; season with salt and black pepper.

2. Place meat mixture on cutting board; pat evenly into 8×6-inch rectangle. With sharp knife, cut meat into 48 (1-inch) squares; shape each square into small oblong sausage.

3. Place sausages on waxed paper-lined jelly-roll pan and freeze 30 to 45 minutes or until firm. Do not freeze completely. Meanwhile, prepare grill for direct cooking.

4. Alternately thread 3 sausages and 3 bell pepper pieces onto each metal skewer.

5. Grill over medium-hot coals 5 to 7 minutes. Turn kabobs, taking care not to knock sausages off. Continue grilling 5 to 7 minutes longer until meat is done. Serve with rice pilaf.

6. For green onion brushes, trim root and most of green tops from green onions. Using sharp scissors, make parallel cuts, about 1½ inches long, along length of each onion at the root end or both ends. Fan out the cuts to form a brush. If desired, place brushes in bowl of ice water for several hours to open and curl. Place green onion brush and several tomato slices on each plate, if desired.

Makes 8 servings or 16 kabobs

Note: The seasonings can be adjusted, but the key to authenticity is the equal parts of beef and lamb and the garlic and paprika. You may use sweet paprika if you prefer a milder taste.

Serbian Lamb Sausage Kabobs

Jamaican Pork Chops with Tropical Fruit Salsa

⅔ cup prepared Italian salad dressing
⅓ cup *Frank's® RedHot®* Original Cayenne Pepper Sauce
⅓ cup lime juice
2 tablespoons brown sugar
2 teaspoons dried thyme leaves
1 teaspoon ground allspice
½ teaspoon ground nutmeg
½ teaspoon ground cinnamon
6 loin pork chops, cut 1 inch thick (about 2½ pounds)
Tropical Fruit Salsa (recipe follows)

Place salad dressing, **Frank's RedHot** Sauce, lime juice, sugar and seasonings in blender or food processor. Cover and process until smooth. Reserve ½ cup dressing mixture for Tropical Fruit Salsa. Place pork chops in large resealable plastic food storage bag. Pour remaining dressing mixture over chops. Seal bag and marinate in refrigerator 1 hour.

Place chops on grid, reserving dressing mixture. Grill over medium coals 30 minutes or until pork is juicy and barely pink in center, turning and basting frequently with dressing mixture. (Do not baste during last 5 minutes of cooking.) Serve chops with Tropical Fruit Salsa. Garnish as desired. *Makes 6 servings*

Tropical Fruit Salsa

1 cup finely chopped fresh pineapple
1 ripe mango, peeled, seeded and finely chopped
2 tablespoons finely chopped red onion
1 tablespoon minced fresh cilantro leaves

Combine pineapple, mango, onion, cilantro and reserved ½ cup dressing mixture in small bowl. Refrigerate until chilled. *Makes about 2½ cups*

Prep Time: 20 minutes
Marinate Time: 1 hour
Cook Time: 30 minutes

Jamaican Pork Chop with Tropical Fruit Salsa

Grilled Chicken with
Spicy Black Beans & Rice

1 boneless skinless chicken breast (about 4 ounces)
½ teaspoon jerk seasoning
½ teaspoon olive oil
¼ cup finely diced green bell pepper
2 teaspoons minced chipotle pepper
¾ cup hot cooked rice
½ cup canned rinsed and drained black beans
2 tablespoons diced pimiento
1 tablespoon chopped pimiento-stuffed green olives
1 tablespoon chopped onion
1 tablespoon chopped fresh cilantro (optional)
Lime wedges

1. Rub chicken with jerk seasonings. Grill over medium-hot coals 8 to 10 minutes or until no longer pink in center.

2. Meanwhile, heat oil in medium saucepan or skillet over medium heat. Add bell pepper and chipotle pepper; cook 7 to 8 minutes, stirring frequently, until peppers are soft.

3. Add rice, beans, pimiento and olives to saucepan. Cook until hot, about 3 minutes.

4. Serve bean mixture with chicken. Top bean mixture with onion and cilantro, if desired. Garnish with lime wedges. *Makes 2 servings*

Grilled Chicken with Spicy Black Beans & Rice

Japanese Yakitori

1 pound boneless skinless chicken breast halves, cut into ¾-inch-wide strips
2 tablespoons sherry or pineapple juice
2 tablespoons reduced-sodium soy sauce
1 tablespoon sugar
1 tablespoon peanut oil
½ teaspoon minced garlic
½ teaspoon minced ginger
5 ounces red pearl onions
½ fresh pineapple, cut into 1-inch wedges

1. Place chicken in large heavy-duty resealable plastic food storage bag. Combine sherry, soy sauce, sugar, oil, garlic and ginger in small bowl; mix thoroughly to dissolve sugar. Pour into plastic bag with chicken; seal bag and turn to coat thoroughly. Refrigerate 30 minutes or up to 2 hours, turning occasionally. (If using wooden or bamboo skewers, soak them in water 20 to 30 minutes to keep from burning.)

2. Meanwhile, place onions in boiling water for 4 minutes; drain and cool in ice water to stop cooking. Cut off root ends and slip off outer skins; set aside.

3. Drain chicken, reserving marinade. Weave chicken accordion-style onto skewers, alternating onions and pineapple with chicken. Brush with reserved marinade; discard remaining marinade.

4. Grill on uncovered grill over medium-hot coals 6 to 8 minutes or until chicken is no longer pink in center, turning once.   *Makes 6 servings*

Japanese Yakitori

Vietnamese Grilled Steak Wraps

    1 beef flank steak (about 1½ pounds)
      Grated peel and juice of 2 lemons
    6 tablespoons sugar, divided
    2 tablespoons dark sesame oil
 1¼ teaspoons salt, divided
    ½ teaspoon black pepper
    ¼ cup water
    ¼ cup rice vinegar
    ½ teaspoon crushed red pepper
    6 (8-inch) flour tortillas
    6 red leaf lettuce leaves
    ⅓ cup lightly packed fresh mint leaves
    ⅓ cup lightly packed fresh cilantro leaves
      Star fruit slices, red bell pepper strips and orange peel strips
      (optional)

Cut beef across the grain into thin slices. Combine lemon peel, juice, 2 tablespoons sugar, sesame oil, 1 teaspoon salt and black pepper in medium bowl. Add beef; toss to coat. Cover and refrigerate at least 30 minutes. Combine water, vinegar, remaining 4 tablespoons sugar and ¼ teaspoon salt in small saucepan; bring to a boil. Boil 5 minutes without stirring until syrupy. Stir in crushed red pepper; set aside.

Remove beef from marinade; discard marinade. Thread beef onto metal or wooden skewers. (Soak wooden skewers in hot water 30 minutes to prevent burning.) Grill beef over medium-hot KINGSFORD® Briquets about 3 minutes per side until cooked through. Grill tortillas until hot. Place lettuce, beef, mint and cilantro on tortillas; drizzle with vinegar mixture. Roll tortillas to enclose filling. Garnish with star fruit, bell pepper and orange peel strips, if desired. *Makes 6 wraps*

Vietnamese Grilled Steak Wrap

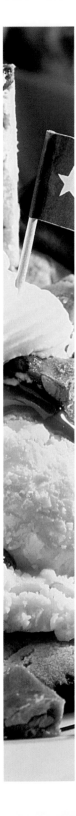

The Party Grill

Hot Wings with Creamy Cool Dipping Sauce

    Creamy Cool Dipping Sauce (recipe follows)
  ¼ **cup chopped onion**
   2 **tablespoons olive oil**
   2 **cloves garlic, minced**
1½ **cups prepared barbecue sauce**
   2 **to 3 teaspoons hot pepper sauce**
   4 **pounds chicken wings (about 16 to 20 wings)**

1. Prepare grill for direct cooking.

2. Prepare Creamy Cool Dipping Sauce; set aside.

3. Place onion, oil and garlic in medium microwavable bowl. Microwave at HIGH 1½ to 2 minutes or until onion is tender. Add barbecue sauce and pepper sauce; stir until blended. Set aside.

4. Place chicken on grid. Grill, covered, over medium-high heat 25 minutes or until chicken is no longer pink and juices run clear, turning after 15 minutes. Turn and brush with barbecue sauce mixture frequently during last 5 minutes of cooking time. Serve with Creamy Cool Dipping Sauce.

Makes 4 main-dish or 8 appetizer servings

Creamy Cool Dipping Sauce

  ⅔ **cup low-fat mayonnaise**
  ¼ **cup ranch-style salad dressing**
   3 **ounces crumbled feta cheese**
   2 **teaspoons finely chopped green onion**

Combine mayonnaise and salad dressing in small bowl. Stir in cheese and onion. Cover and refrigerate until serving. *Makes about 1¼ cups*

Hot Wings with Creamy Cool Dipping Sauce

Beef Tenderloin with Dijon-Cream Sauce

3 tablespoons balsamic vinegar*
2 tablespoons olive oil
1 beef tenderloin roast (about 1½ to 2 pounds)
  Salt
3 tablespoons mustard seeds
1½ tablespoons white peppercorns
1½ tablespoons black peppercorns
  Dijon-Cream Sauce (recipe follows)

*Substitute 2 tablespoons red wine vinegar plus 1½ teaspoons sugar for the balsamic vinegar.

Combine vinegar and oil in a cup; rub onto beef. Season generously with salt. Let stand 15 minutes. Meanwhile, coarsely crush mustard seeds and peppercorns in a blender or food processor or by hand with a mortar and pestle. Roll beef in crushed mixture, pressing it into the surface to coat.

Oil hot grid to help prevent sticking. Grill beef, on a covered grill, over medium KINGSFORD® Briquets, 16 to 24 minutes (depending on size and thickness) until a meat thermometer inserted in the center almost registers 145°F for medium-rare. (Cook until 160°F for medium or 170°F well done; add another 5 minutes for every 10°F.) Turn halfway through cooking. Let stand 5 to 10 minutes before slicing. Slice and serve with a few spoonfuls of sauce.   *Makes 6 servings*

Dijon-Cream Sauce

1 can (14½ ounces) beef broth
1 cup whipping cream
2 tablespoons butter, softened
1½ to 2 tablespoons Dijon mustard
1 to 1½ tablespoons balsamic vinegar*
  Coarsely crushed black peppercorns and mustard seeds for garnish

*Substitute 2 teaspoons red wine vinegar plus 1 teaspoon sugar for the balsamic vinegar.

Bring beef broth and whipping cream to a boil in a saucepan. Boil gently until reduced to about 1 cup; sauce will be thick enough to coat a spoon. Remove from heat; stir in butter, a little at a time, until all the butter is melted. Stir in mustard and vinegar, adjusting amounts to taste. Sprinkle with peppercorns and mustard seeds.

Makes about 1 cup

Beef Tenderloin with Dijon-Cream Sauce

Mesquite-Grilled Turkey

2 cups mesquite chips, divided
1 fresh or thawed frozen turkey (10 to 12 pounds)
1 small sweet or Spanish onion, peeled and quartered
1 lemon, quartered
10 fresh tarragon sprigs, divided
2 tablespoons butter or margarine, softened
  Salt and pepper (optional)
¼ cup butter or margarine, melted
2 tablespoons fresh lemon juice
2 tablespoons chopped fresh tarragon leaves *or* 2 teaspoons dried
   tarragon leaves, crushed
2 cloves garlic, minced

1. Cover mesquite chips with cold water; soak 20 minutes. Prepare grill for indirect cooking. Rinse turkey; pat dry with paper towels. Place onion, lemon and 3 tarragon sprigs in cavity. Pull skin over neck; secure with metal skewer. Tuck wing tips under back; tie legs together with wet kitchen string.

2. Spread softened butter over turkey skin; sprinkle with salt and pepper, if desired. Insert meat thermometer into center of thickest part of thigh, not touching bone.

3. Drain mesquite chips; sprinkle 1 cup over coals. Place turkey, breast side up, on grid directly over drip pan. Grill turkey, on covered grill, over medium coals 11 to 14 minutes per pound, adding 4 to 9 briquets to both sides of fire each hour to maintain medium coals and adding remaining 1 cup mesquite chips after 1 hour of grilling. Meanwhile, soak remaining fresh tarragon sprigs in water.

4. Combine melted butter, lemon juice, chopped tarragon and garlic in small bowl. Brush half of mixture over turkey during last 30 minutes of grilling. Place soaked tarragon sprigs directly on coals. Continue to grill, covered, 20 minutes. Brush with remaining mixture. Continue to grill, covered, about 10 minutes or until thermometer registers 185°F.

6. Transfer turkey to carving board; tent with foil. Let stand 15 minutes before carving. Discard onion, lemon and tarragon sprigs from cavity.

Makes 8 to 10 servings

Mesquite-Grilled Turkey

Lobster Tail with Tasty Butters

Hot & Spicy Butter, Scallion Butter or Chili-Mustard Butter (recipes follow)
4 fresh or thawed frozen lobster tails (about 5 ounces each)

1. Prepare grill for direct cooking. Prepare choice of butter mixture.

2. Rinse lobster tails in cold water. Butterfly tails by cutting lengthwise through centers of hard top shells and meat. Cut to, but not through, bottoms of shells. Press shell halves of tails apart with fingers. Brush lobster meat with butter mixture.

3. Place tails on grid, meat side down. Grill, uncovered, over medium-high heat 4 minutes. Turn tails meat side up. Brush with butter mixture; grill 4 to 5 minutes or until lobster meat turns opaque.

4. Heat remaining butter mixture, stirring occasionally. Serve butter mixture for dipping. *Makes 4 servings*

Tasty Butters

Hot & Spicy Butter
   1/3 **cup butter or margarine, melted**
   1 **tablespoon chopped onion**
   2 to 3 **teaspoons hot pepper sauce**
   1 **teaspoon dried thyme leaves**
   1/4 **teaspoon ground allspice**

Scallion Butter
   1/3 **cup butter or margarine, melted**
   1 **tablespoon finely chopped green onion tops**
   1 **tablespoon lemon juice**
   1 **teaspoon grated lemon peel**
   1/4 **teaspoon black pepper**

Chili-Mustard Butter
   1/3 **cup butter or margarine, melted**
   1 **tablespoon chopped onion**
   1 **tablespoon Dijon mustard**
   1 **teaspoon chili powder**

For each butter sauce, combine ingredients in small bowl.

Lobster Tail with Hot & Spicy Butter

Chocolate-Caramel S'Mores

12 chocolate wafer cookies or chocolate graham cracker squares
2 tablespoons caramel ice cream topping
6 large marshmallows

1. Prepare coals for grilling. Place 6 wafer cookies top sides down on plate. Spread 1 teaspoon caramel topping in center of each wafer to within about ¼ inch of edge.

2. Spear 1 to 2 marshmallows onto long wood-handled skewer.* Hold several inches above coals 3 to 5 minutes or until marshmallows are golden and very soft, turning slowly. Push 1 marshmallow off into center of caramel. Top with plain wafer. Repeat with remaining marshmallows and wafers. *Makes 6 servings*

*If wood-handled skewers are unavailable, use oven mitt to protect hand from heat.

Tip: S'Mores, a favorite campfire treat, got their name because everyone who tasted them wanted "some more." In the unlikely event of leftover S'Mores, they can be reheated in the microwave at HIGH 5 to 10 seconds.

Half of all marshmallows eaten in the U.S. have been toasted over a grill.

Chocolate-Caramel S'Mores

Cowboy Burgers

1 pound ground beef or turkey
½ teaspoon LAWRY'S® Seasoned Salt
½ teaspoon LAWRY'S® Seasoned Pepper
3 tablespoons butter or margarine
1 large onion, thinly sliced
1 package (1 ounce) LAWRY'S® Taco Spices & Seasonings
4 slices cheddar cheese
4 Kaiser rolls
   Lettuce leaves
   Tomato slices

In medium bowl, combine ground beef, Seasoned Salt and Seasoned Pepper; shape into four patties. Grill or broil to desired doneness. Meanwhile, in medium skillet, melt butter. Mix in onion and Taco Spices & Seasoning. Cook onion until soft and transparent. Top each patty with onion and cheese. Return to grill or broiler until cheese is melted. Place each patty on roll; top with lettuce and tomato.

Makes 4 servings

Meal Idea: Serve with your favorite baked beans.

Prep. Time 5 minutes
Cook Time: 7 to 10 minutes

Cowboy Burger

Bold and Zesty Beef Back Ribs

5 pounds beef back ribs, cut into 3- or 4-rib sections
Salt and black pepper
1 teaspoon vegetable oil
1 small onion, minced
2 cloves garlic, minced
1 cup ketchup
½ cup chili sauce
2 tablespoons lemon juice
1 tablespoon packed brown sugar
1 teaspoon hot pepper sauce

1. Place ribs in shallow pan; season with salt and pepper. Keep refrigerated until ready to grill.

2. Prepare grill for indirect cooking. While coals are heating, prepare barbecue sauce.

3. Heat oil in large nonstick saucepan over medium heat until hot. Add onion and garlic. Cook and stir 5 minutes or until onion is tender. Stir in remaining ingredients. Reduce heat to medium-low; cook 15 minutes, stirring occasionally.

4. Baste ribs generously with sauce; grill 45 to 60 minutes or until ribs are tender and browned, turning occasionally.

5. Bring remaining sauce to a boil over medium-high heat; boil 1 minute. Serve ribs with remaining sauce.   *Makes 5 to 6 servings*

Prep Time: 15 minutes
Cook Time: 55 minutes to 1 hour 15 minutes

Bold and Zesty Beef Back Ribs

Jamaican Rum Chicken

½ cup dark rum
2 tablespoons lime juice or lemon juice
2 tablespoons soy sauce
2 tablespoons brown sugar
4 large cloves garlic, minced
1 to 2 jalapeño peppers,* seeded and minced
1 tablespoon minced fresh ginger
1 teaspoon dried thyme leaves, crushed
½ teaspoon black pepper
6 boneless skinless chicken breast halves

*Jalapeño peppers can sting and irritate the skin; wear rubber gloves when handling peppers and do not touch eyes. Wash hands after handling.

1. To prepare marinade, combine rum, lime juice, soy sauce, sugar, garlic, chilies, ginger, thyme and black pepper in small bowl.

2. Rinse chicken and pat dry with paper towels. Place chicken in resealable plastic food storage bag; pour marinade over chicken. Press air out of bag and seal tightly. Turn bag over to completely coat chicken with marinade. Refrigerate 4 hours or overnight, turning bag once or twice.

3. Prepare grill for direct grilling by spreading hot coals in single layer that extends 1 to 2 inches beyond area of food.

4. Drain chicken; reserve marinade. Place chicken on grid. Grill chicken, on uncovered grill, over medium-hot coals 6 minutes per side or until chicken is no longer pink in center.

5. Meanwhile, bring remaining marinade to a boil in small saucepan over medium-high heat. Boil 5 minutes or until marinade is reduced by about half.

6. To serve, drizzle marinade over chicken. Garnish as desired.

Makes 6 servings

Jamaican Rum Chicken

Grilled Garlic & Herb Pizzas

Homemade Pizza Dough (page 200)
8 cloves Grilled Garlic (page 200)
1 medium yellow onion
Olive oil
1 medium red, yellow or orange bell pepper
1 cup crumbled goat cheese
¼ cup chopped fresh herb mixture (thyme, basil, oregano and parsley) *or* 4 teaspoons dry herb mixture
¼ cup grated Parmesan cheese

Prepare Homemade Pizza Dough. While dough is rising, light KINGSFORD® Briquets in covered grill. Arrange medium-hot briquets on one side of the grill. Prepare Grilled Garlic. Lightly oil grid to prevent sticking. Cut onion into ½-inch-thick slices. Insert wooden picks into onion slices from edges to prevent separating into rings. (Soak wooden picks in hot water 15 minutes to prevent burning.) Brush onion lightly with oil. Place whole bell pepper and onion slices on grid around edge of briquets. Grill, covered, 20 to 30 minutes until tender, turning once or twice. Remove picks from onion slices and separate into rings. Cut pepper in half and remove seeds when cool enough to handle; slice pepper halves into strips.

Roll or gently stretch each ball of dough into 7-inch round. Brush lightly with oil on both sides. Grill dough on grid directly above medium-hot KINGSFORD® Briquets 1 to 3 minutes or until dough starts to bubble and bottom is lightly browned. Turn; grill 3 to 5 minutes or until second side is lightly browned and dough is cooked through. Remove from grill. Spread 2 cloves Grilled Garlic onto each crust; top with onion rings, pepper strips, goat cheese, herbs and Parmesan cheese, dividing equally. Place pizzas around edge of coals; grill covered 5 minutes until bottom crust is crisp, cheese melts and toppings are heated through.

Makes 4 individual pizzas

Note: A 1-pound loaf of frozen bread dough, thawed, can be substituted for Homemade Pizza Dough. Or, substitute 4 pre-baked individual Italian bread shells, add toppings and warm on the grill.

continued on page 200

Grilled Garlic & Herb Pizzas

Grilled Garlic & Herb Pizzas, *continued*

Homemade Pizza Dough

2¾ cups all-purpose flour, divided
  1 package quick-rising yeast
  ¾ teaspoon salt
  1 cup water
1½ tablespoons vegetable oil

Combine 1½ cups flour, yeast and salt in food processor. Heat water and oil in small saucepan until 120° to 130°F. With food processor running, add water and oil to flour mixture; process 30 seconds. Add 1 cup flour; process until dough comes together to form ball. Knead on floured board 3 to 4 minutes or until smooth and satiny, kneading in as much of the remaining ¼ cup flour as needed to prevent dough from sticking. Place dough in oiled bowl, turning once. Cover with towel; let rise in warm place 30 minutes until doubled in bulk. Divide dough into 4 equal balls.

Grilled Garlic

1 or 2 heads garlic
  Olive oil

Peel outermost papery skin from garlic heads. Brush heads with oil. Grill heads at edge of grid on covered grill over medium-hot KINGSFORD® Briquets 30 to 45 minutes or until cloves are soft and buttery. Remove from grill; cool slightly. Gently squeeze softened garlic heads from root end so that cloves slip out of skins into small bowl. Use immediately or cover and refrigerate up to 1 week.

Spicy Apricot Sesame Wings

⅓ cup *Frank's® RedHot®* Original Cayenne Pepper Sauce
½ cup *French's®* Honey Dijon Mustard
2 tablespoons Asian sesame oil
1 tablespoon red wine vinegar
½ cup apricot jam
2 pounds chicken wings, split and tips discarded
2 tablespoons toasted sesame seeds*

To toast sesame seeds, place on baking sheet and bake at 375°F 8 to 10 minutes or until golden.

1. Stir **Frank's RedHot** Sauce, mustard, sesame oil and vinegar in small measuring cup. Spoon ¼ cup **Frank's RedHot** Sauce mixture and apricot jam into blender or food processor. Cover; process until smooth. Reserve for basting and dipping sauce.

2. Place wings in large bowl. Pour remaining **Frank's RedHot** Sauce mixture over wings; toss to coat. Cover; marinate in refrigerator 20 minutes.

3. Place wings on oiled grid and discard any remaining marinade. Grill over medium heat 25 to 30 minutes or until crispy and no longer pink, turning often. Brush with ¼ cup of sauce during last 10 minutes of cooking. Place wings on serving platter; sprinkle with sesame seeds. Serve with remaining sauce.   *Makes 8 servings*

Prep Time: 15 minutes
Marinate Time: 20 minutes
Cook Time: 25 minutes

Hawaiian Shrimp Kabobs

1 can (6 ounces) pineapple juice
⅓ cup packed brown sugar
4 teaspoons cornstarch
1 tablespoon rice vinegar
1 tablespoon reduced-sodium soy sauce
1 clove garlic, minced
¼ teaspoon ground ginger
1 medium-size green bell pepper
1 medium-size red bell pepper
1 medium onion
1 cup fresh pineapple chunks
1 cup fresh mango or papaya chunks
1 pound raw large shrimp, peeled and deveined
2½ cups hot cooked white rice
Red onion rings and fresh herb sprigs (optional)

1. For sauce, combine juice, sugar, cornstarch, vinegar, soy sauce, garlic and ginger in saucepan. Cook over medium-high heat until mixture comes to a boil and thickens, stirring frequently; set aside.

2. Prepare grill for direct cooking. Cut peppers and onion into 1-inch squares. Thread peppers, onion, pineapple, mango and shrimp onto 10 metal skewers. Place kabobs in large glass baking dish. Brush sauce over kabobs.

3. Place kabobs on grid. Grill 3 to 4 minutes. Turn and brush with sauce; discard any remaining sauce. Grill 3 to 4 minutes more or until shrimp turn pink and opaque. Serve with rice. Garnish with onion rings and herbs, if desired.

Makes 5 servings

Hawaiian Shrimp Kabobs

Barbecued Chicken with Chili-Orange Glaze

1 to 2 dried chili peppers (de arbol or other variety)*
½ cup fresh orange juice
2 tablespoons tequila
2 cloves garlic, minced
1½ teaspoons grated orange peel
¼ teaspoon salt
¼ cup vegetable oil
1 broiler-fryer chicken (about 3 pounds), cut into quarters
Orange slices (optional)
Cilantro sprigs (optional)

*For milder flavor, discard seeds from chili peppers. Since chili peppers can sting and irritate the skin, wear rubber gloves when handling peppers and do not touch eyes. Wash hands after handling chili peppers.

1. Crush chilies into coarse flakes in mortar with pestle. Combine chilies, orange juice, tequila, garlic, orange peel and salt in small bowl. Gradually add oil, whisking continuously, until marinade is thoroughly blended.

2. Arrange chicken in single layer in shallow glass baking dish. Pour marinade over chicken; turn pieces to coat. Marinate, covered, in refrigerator 2 to 3 hours, turning chicken and basting with marinade several times.

3. Prepare charcoal grill for direct cooking or preheat broiler. Drain chicken, reserving marinade. Bring marinade to a boil in small saucepan over high heat; boil 2 minutes. Grill chicken on covered grill or broil, 6 to 8 inches from heat, 15 minutes, brushing frequently with marinade. Turn chicken. Grill or broil 15 minutes more or until chicken is no longer pink in center and juices run clear, brushing frequently with marinade. *Do not baste during last 5 minutes of grilling.* Discard remaining marinade. Garnish with orange slices and cilantro, if desired. *Makes 4 servings*

Barbecued Chicken with Chili-Orange Glaze

Ginger Beef and Pineapple Kabobs

1 cup LAWRY'S® Thai Ginger Marinade With Lime Juice, divided
1 can (16 ounces) pineapple chunks, juice reserved
1½ pounds boneless beef top sirloin steak, cut into 1½-inch cubes
2 red bell peppers, cut into chunks
2 medium onions, cut into wedges

In large resealable plastic food storage bag, combine ½ cup Thai Ginger Marinade and 1 tablespoon pineapple juice; mix well. Add steak, bell peppers and onions; seal bag. Marinate in refrigerator at least 30 minutes. Remove steak and vegetables; discard used marinade. Alternately thread steak, vegetables and pineapple onto skewers. Grill or broil skewers 10 to 15 minutes or until desired doneness, turning once and basting often with additional ½ cup Thai Ginger Marinade. Do not baste during last 5 minutes of cooking. Discard any remaining marinade.

Makes 6 servings

Serving Suggestion: Serve kabobs with a light salad and bread.

The word "barbecue" probably comes from the Mayan word "barbacoa" which referred to the lattice of green wood on which foods were placed for cooking over coals.

Ginger Beef and Pineapple Kabobs

Grilled Quesadilla Snacks

1½ cups (6 ounces) shredded Monterey Jack cheese
½ red or yellow bell pepper, chopped
2 ounces sliced smoked ham, cut into thin strips
2 ounces sliced smoked turkey, cut into thin strips
¼ cup finely chopped green onions
⅓ cup French's® Classic Yellow® Mustard
2 teaspoons ground cumin
10 flour tortillas (6 inch)

1. Combine cheese, bell pepper, ham, turkey and onions in medium bowl. Combine mustard and cumin in small bowl; mix well.

2. Place 5 tortillas on sheet of waxed paper. Spread 1 rounded teaspoon mustard mixture over each tortilla. Sprinkle cheese mixture evenly over mustard mixture. Top with another tortilla, pressing down firmly to form quesadilla.

3. Place quesadillas on oiled grid. Grill over medium heat 2 minutes or until cheese is melted and quesadillas are heated through, turning once. Cut each quesadilla into quarters. Serve with salsa and cilantro, if desired. *Makes 10 servings*

Prep Time: 30 minutes
Cook Time: 2 minutes

Grilled Quesadilla Snacks

Chicken Satay

1 pound boneless skinless chicken breast halves
1 recipe Peanut Dip (recipe follows), divided
Cucumber slices
Chopped fresh cilantro

1. Soak 8 (6-inch) bamboo skewers in hot water 20 minutes. Cut chicken lengthwise into 1-inch-wide strips; thread onto skewers.

2. Place skewers in large shallow glass dish. Pour ½ cup Peanut Dip over chicken, turning to coat evenly. Cover and marinate in refrigerator 30 minutes.

3. Place skewers on oiled grid and discard any remaining marinade. Grill over high heat 5 to 8 minutes or until chicken is no longer pink, turning once. Place on serving platter. Serve with cucumber, cilantro and remaining Peanut Dip.

Makes 8 appetizer or 4 main-dish servings

Prep Time: 15 minutes
Marinate Time: 30 minutes
Cook Time: 5 minutes

Peanut Dip

⅓ cup peanut butter
⅓ cup French's® Honey Dijon Mustard
⅓ cup orange juice
1 tablespoon chopped peeled fresh ginger
1 tablespoon honey
1 tablespoon Frank's® RedHot® Original Cayenne Pepper Sauce
1 tablespoon teriyaki baste and glaze sauce
2 cloves garlic, minced

Combine peanut butter, mustard, juice, ginger, honey, **Frank's RedHot** Sauce, teriyaki baste and glaze sauce and garlic in large bowl. Refrigerate until ready to serve.

Makes 1 cup dip

Tip: Serve Peanut Dip with Chicken Satay or as a dip for assorted cut-up fresh vegetables. It is also great as a spread on grilled French bread with grilled vegetables.

Prep Time: 10 minutes

Chicken Satay and Peanut Dip

Fajita-Style Beef Wraps

1 package (1.27 ounces) LAWRY'S® Fajita Spices & Seasonings
2 tablespoons vegetable oil
½ pound top sirloin steak
½ cup chopped green bell pepper
1 cup thinly sliced red onion
1 can (8¾ ounces) garbanzo beans, drained
1 tomato, quartered and thinly sliced
8 large (burrito size) *or* 12 small (soft taco size) flour tortillas,
**   warmed to soften**

In small bowl, mix together Fajita Spices & Seasonings and oil. Spread 1 teaspoon of seasoning paste evenly over each side of steak. If a more intense flavor is desired, cover and refrigerate steak 30 minutes before grilling or broiling. Set aside remaining seasoning paste. Grill or broil meat to desired doneness. Slice into thin strips. In large bowl, combine green pepper, onion, garbanzo beans, tomato, steak and remaining seasoning paste; stir to coat evenly. Scoop ½ to ⅓ cup beef mixture onto each tortilla. Fold in sides and roll up to enclose filling. Wrap each burrito in plastic wrap and refrigerate until ready to serve or transport to picnic.

Makes 8 large or 12 small wraps

Hint: Filling may be prepared the night before then wrapped in tortillas the next day or at the picnic!

Prep Time: 10 to 15 minutes
Cook Time: 8 to 10 minutes

Fajita-Style Beef Wraps

The Vegetable Grill

Grilled Vegetable Platter

1 cup LAWRY'S® Herb & Garlic Marinade With Lemon Juice
12 small portabello mushrooms, cut into ½-inch slices
2 zucchini or yellow squash, cut into ½-inch slices
1 small onion, cut into wedges
1 small Japanese eggplant, cut into ½-inch slices
2 red, green and/or yellow bell peppers, cut into chunks

In large resealable plastic bag, combine all ingredients; mix well. Seal bag and marinate in refrigerator at least 30 minutes. Remove vegetables; reserve used marinade. Grill or broil mixed vegetables 10 to 12 minutes or until tender (mushrooms cook quickly), turning once and brushing often with reserved marinade. Vegetables should be slightly "charred." Arrange vegetables on platter.

Makes 6 servings

Meal Idea: A great recipe to take along as a picnic side dish, to top a main-dish salad, to wrap up in a tortilla or to add to a sandwich. Can be made ahead and kept in refrigerator until ready to use. Serve warm, cold or at room temperature!

Variation: Place vegetables on skewers and grill over medium heat to desired doneness.

Hint: For oven roasting, preheat oven to 450°F. If roasting root vegetables, cover and roast 20 minutes. Uncover and continue roasting 20 to 25 minutes, or until tender.

Prep Time: 10 minutes
Marinating Time: 30 minutes
Cook Time: 10 to 12 minutes

Grilled Vegetable Platter

Buffalo Chili Onions

½ cup *Frank's*® *RedHot*® Original Cayenne Pepper Sauce
½ cup (1 stick) butter or margarine, melted or olive oil
¼ cup chili sauce
1 tablespoon chili powder
4 large sweet onions, cut into ½-inch-thick slices

Whisk together ***Frank's RedHot*** Sauce, butter, chili sauce and chili powder in medium bowl until blended; brush on onion slices.

Place onions on grid. Grill over medium-high coals 10 minutes or until tender, turning and basting often with the chili mixture. Serve warm.   *Makes 6 side-dish servings*

Tip: Onions may be prepared ahead and grilled just before serving.

Prep Time: 10 minutes
Cook Time: 10 minutes

Some barbecue pit masters use full size floor mops to apply basting liquid to meat as it cooks. They use brand-new mops, of course.

Buffalo Chili Onions

Grilled Cajun Potato Wedges

3 large russet potatoes, washed, scrubbed and unpeeled (about 2¼ pounds)
¼ cup olive oil
2 cloves garlic, minced
1 teaspoon salt
1 teaspoon paprika
½ teaspoon dried thyme leaves
½ teaspoon dried oregano leaves
¼ teaspoon black pepper
⅛ to ¼ teaspoon ground red pepper
2 cups mesquite chips

1. Prepare grill for direct cooking. Preheat oven to 425°F.

2. Cut potatoes in half lengthwise; then cut each half lengthwise into 4 wedges. Place potatoes in large bowl. Add oil and garlic; toss to coat well.

3. Combine salt, paprika, thyme, oregano, black pepper and ground red pepper in small bowl. Sprinkle over potatoes; toss to coat well. Place potato wedges in single layer in shallow roasting pan. (Reserve remaining oil mixture left in large bowl.) Bake 20 minutes.

4. Meanwhile, cover mesquite chips with cold water; soak 20 minutes. Drain mesquite chips; sprinkle over coals. Place potato wedges on their sides on grid. Grill potato wedges, on covered grill, over medium coals 15 to 20 minutes or until potatoes are browned and fork-tender, brushing with reserved oil mixture halfway through grilling time and turning once with tongs.   *Makes 4 to 6 servings*

Grilled Cajun Potato Wedges

Pinto Burgers

1 (15-ounce) can pinto beans, drained and rinsed
1 egg
1 medium carrot, peeled and grated
¼ cup minced red bell pepper
1 large green onion, minced
2 teaspoons TABASCO® brand Pepper Sauce
1 teaspoon salt
1 tablespoon vegetable oil
3 whole wheat rolls, split
    Vegetable toppings such as spinach leaves, alfalfa or radish
      sprouts, sliced red onion, cherry tomatoes (optional)

Preheat grill or broiler. Mash beans in large bowl with potato masher until most beans are crushed. (Or process beans in food processor.) Add egg, carrot, red bell pepper, green onion, TABASCO® Sauce and salt; stir until well blended. Shape into three ¾-inch-thick patties.

Spray burgers with nonstick cooking spray. Grill or broil 4 to 6 inches from heat source for about 3 minutes on each side. To serve, place burgers on bottom halves of rolls; top with desired vegetable toppings and remaining roll halves.

Makes 3 servings

Pinto Burger

BBQ Corn Wheels

4 ears corn on the cob, husked and cleaned
3 red, green or yellow bell peppers, cut into large chunks
¾ cup barbecue sauce
½ cup honey
¼ cup *French's*® Worcestershire Sauce
Vegetable cooking spray

1. Cut corn into ½-inch slices. Alternately thread corn and pepper chunks onto four metal skewers. (Pierce tip of skewer through center of corn wheel to thread.) Combine barbecue sauce, honey and Worcestershire.

2. Coat kabobs with vegetable cooking spray. Grill kabobs on greased rack over medium heat for 5 minutes. Cook 5 minutes more until corn is tender, turning and basting with barbecue sauce mixture. Serve any extra sauce on the side with grilled hamburgers, steaks or chicken. *Makes 4 servings*

Prep Time: 10 minutes
Cook Time: 10 minutes

The oldest barbecue restaurant in the U.S. is Tadich Grill in San Francisco which opened in 1849.

BBQ Corn Wheels

Honey-Grilled Vegetables

12 small red potatoes, halved
¼ cup honey
3 tablespoons dry white wine
1 clove garlic, minced
1 teaspoon dried thyme, crushed
½ teaspoon salt
½ teaspoon black pepper
2 zucchini, halved lengthwise and cut crosswise into halves
1 medium eggplant, sliced ½ inch thick
1 green bell pepper, cut vertically in eighths
1 red bell pepper, cut vertically in eighths
1 large onion, sliced ½ inch thick

Cover potatoes with water. Bring to a boil and simmer 5 minutes; drain. Combine honey, wine, garlic, thyme, salt and black pepper; mix well. Place vegetables on oiled barbecue grill over hot coals. Grill 20 to 25 minutes, turning and brushing with honey mixture every 7 or 8 minutes.   *Makes 4 to 6 servings*

Oven Method: Toss vegetables with honey mixture. Bake, uncovered, at 400°F 25 minutes or until tender; stir every 8 to 10 minutes to prevent burning.

Favorite recipe from **National Honey Board**

Honey-Grilled Vegetables

Portobello Mushrooms Sesame

4 large portobello mushrooms
2 tablespoons sweet rice wine
2 tablespoons reduced-sodium soy sauce
2 cloves garlic, minced
1 teaspoon dark sesame oil

1. Prepare grill for direct cooking.

2. Remove and discard stems from mushrooms; set caps aside. Combine remaining ingredients in small bowl.

3. Brush both sides of mushroom caps with soy sauce mixture. Grill mushrooms, top sides up, on covered grill over medium coals 3 to 4 minutes. Brush tops with soy sauce mixture; turn over. Grill 2 minutes more or until mushrooms are lightly browned. Turn again and grill, basting frequently, 4 to 5 minutes or until tender when pressed with back of spatula. Remove mushrooms; cut diagonally into ½-inch-thick slices.

Makes 4 servings

Grilled Asparagus and New Potatoes

1 pound small red potatoes, scrubbed and quartered
¼ cup *French's*® Classic Yellow® Mustard or Honey Dijon Mustard
3 tablespoons minced fresh dill *or* 2 teaspoons dried dill weed
3 tablespoons olive oil
3 tablespoons lemon juice
1 tablespoon grated lemon peel
⅛ teaspoon black pepper
1 pound asparagus, washed and trimmed

1. Place potatoes and ¼ cup water in shallow microwavable dish. Cover and microwave on HIGH (100%) 8 minutes or until potatoes are crisp-tender, turning once. Drain.

2. Combine mustard, dill, oil, lemon juice, lemon peel and pepper in small bowl. Brush mixture on potatoes and asparagus. Place vegetables in grilling basket. Grill over medium-high heat 8 minutes or until potatoes and asparagus are fork-tender, turning and basting often with mustard mixture. *Makes 4 servings*

Prep Time: 15 minutes
Cook Time: 16 minutes

Portobello Mushrooms Sesame

Grilled Vegetables & Brown Rice

1 medium zucchini
1 medium red or yellow bell pepper, quartered lengthwise
1 small onion, cut crosswise into 1-inch-thick slices
¾ cup Italian dressing
4 cups hot cooked UNCLE BEN'S® Original Brown Rice

1. Cut zucchini lengthwise into thirds. Place all vegetables in large resealable plastic food storage bag; add dressing. Seal bag; refrigerate several hours or overnight.

2. Remove vegetables from marinade, reserving marinade. Place bell peppers and onion on grill over medium coals; brush with marinade. Grill 5 minutes. Turn vegetables over; add zucchini. Brush with marinade. Continue grilling until vegetables are crisp-tender, about 5 minutes, turning zucchini over after 3 minutes.

3. Remove vegetables from grill; coarsely chop. Add to hot rice; mix lightly. Season with salt and black pepper, if desired. *Makes 6 to 8 servings*

Cook's Tip: Grilling adds a unique smokey flavor to vegetables and brings out their natural sweetness. The easiest way to grill vegetables is to cut them into large pieces and toss them in salad dressing or seasoned oil before grilling. Seasoned raw vegetables may also be wrapped tightly in foil packets and grilled until tender.

Grilled Vegetables & Brown Rice

Grilled Portobello Mushrooms and Summer Squash with Orange Vinaigrette

Orange Vinaigrette
   2 cups freshly squeezed orange juice
   ¼ cup CRISCO® Oil
   2 tablespoons rice wine vinegar
   1 tablespoon cider vinegar
   1 tablespoon fresh grated orange peel
   Salt and black pepper

Vegetables
   4 whole portobello mushrooms, stems removed
   4 thin yellow summer squash, cut lengthwise about ½-inch thick
   ¼ cup CRISCO® Oil
   Salt and black pepper
   Salad greens
   5 scallions, diagonally sliced
   Toasted sesame seeds

For Orange Vinaigrette, bring orange juice to a boil in saucepan over medium-high heat and reduce to about ½ cup. Remove from heat and whisk in CRISCO® Oil, rice wine vinegar, cider vinegar and orange peel. Add salt and pepper to taste. Chill until ready to use.

For vegetables, brush with CRISCO® Oil and season with salt and pepper. Grill over medium-hot coals until vegetables are tender.

To serve, place salad greens on 4 plates. Arrange grilled vegetables on top of greens and drizzle with Orange Vinaigrette. Sprinkle with scallions and sesame seeds.

Makes 4 servings

Grilled Portobello Mushrooms and Summer Squash with Orange Vinaigrette

Grilled Sweet Potatoes

4 medium-sized sweet potatoes (2 pounds), peeled
⅓ cup *French's*® Honey Dijon Mustard
2 tablespoons olive oil
1 tablespoon minced fresh rosemary *or* 1 teaspoon dried rosemary
½ teaspoon salt
¼ teaspoon black pepper

1. Cut potatoes diagonally into ½-inch-thick slices. Place potatoes and 1 cup water in shallow microwavable dish. Cover with vented plastic wrap and microwave on HIGH (100%) 6 minutes or until potatoes are crisp-tender, turning once. (Cook potatoes in two batches, if necessary.) Drain well.

2. Combine mustard, oil, rosemary, salt and pepper in small bowl; brush on potato slices. Place potatoes on oiled grid. Grill over medium-high heat 5 to 8 minutes or until potatoes are fork-tender, turning and basting often with mustard mixture.

Makes 4 servings

Tip: The task of selecting sweet potatoes is an easy one. Just look for medium-sized potatoes with thick, dark orange skins that are free from bruises. Sweet potatoes keep best in a dry, dark area at about 55°F. Under these conditions they should last about 3 to 4 weeks.

Prep Time: 15 minutes
Cook Time: 18 minutes

Grilled Sweet Potatoes

Grilled Coriander Corn

4 ears fresh corn
3 tablespoons butter or margarine, softened
1 teaspoon ground coriander
¼ teaspoon salt
⅛ teaspoon ground red pepper

1. Pull outer husks from top to base of each corn; leave husks attached to ear. (If desired, remove 1 strip of husk from inner portion of each ear; reserve for later use.) Strip away silk from corn.

2. Place corn in large bowl. Cover with cold water; soak 20 to 30 minutes.

3. Meanwhile, prepare grill for direct cooking.

4. Remove corn from water; pat kernels dry with paper towels. Combine butter, coriander, salt and ground red pepper in small bowl. Spread evenly with spatula over kernels.

5. Bring husks back up each ear of corn; secure at top with paper-covered metal twist-ties. (Or, use reserved strips of corn husk to tie knots at the top of each ear, if desired.)

6. Place corn on grid. Grill corn, on covered grill, over medium-hot coals 20 to 25 minutes or until corn is hot and tender, turning halfway through grilling time with tongs. *Makes 4 servings*

Note: For ember cooking, prepare corn as recipe directs, but omit soaking in cold water. Wrap each ear securely in heavy-duty foil. Place directly on coals. Grill corn, in covered grill, on medium-hot coals 25 to 30 minutes or until corn is hot and tender, turning every 10 minutes with tongs.

Grilled Coriander Corn

Grilled Baby Artichokes with Pepper Dip

18 baby artichokes* (about 1½ pounds)
½ teaspoon salt
¼ cup *Frank's*® *RedHot*® Original Cayenne Pepper Sauce
¼ cup butter or margarine, melted
   Roasted Pepper Dip (recipe follows)

*You can substitute 2 packages (9 ounces each) frozen artichoke halves, thawed and drained. Do not microwave. Brush with Frank's® RedHot® butter mixture and grill as directed below.

1. Wash and trim tough outer leaves from artichokes. Cut ½-inch off top of artichokes, then cut in half lengthwise. Place artichoke halves, 1 cup water and salt in 3-quart microwavable bowl. Cover; microwave on HIGH 8 minutes or until just tender. Thread artichoke halves onto metal skewers.

2. Prepare grill. Combine ***Frank's RedHot*** Sauce and butter in small bowl. Brush mixture over artichokes. Place artichokes on grid. Grill, over hot coals, 5 minutes or until tender, turning and basting often with sauce mixture. Serve artichokes with Roasted Pepper Dip.   *Makes 6 servings*

Prep Time: 20 minutes
Cook Time: 13 minutes

Roasted Pepper Dip

1 jar (7 ounces) roasted red peppers, drained
1 clove garlic, chopped
¼ cup reduced-fat mayonnaise
2 tablespoons *French's*® Honey Dijon Mustard
2 tablespoons *Frank's*® *RedHot*® Original Cayenne Pepper Sauce
¼ teaspoon salt

1. Place roasted peppers and garlic in food processor or blender. Cover; process on high until very smooth.

2. Add mayonnaise, mustard, ***Frank's RedHot*** Sauce and salt. Process until well blended. Cover; refrigerate 30 minutes.   *Makes about 1 cup*

Prep Time: 10 minutes
Chill Time: 30 minutes

Grilled Baby Artichokes with Pepper Dip

Fire-Roasted Tomatoes with Gemelli Pasta

4 pounds Roma tomatoes
12 ounces uncooked gemelli, penne, or fusilli pasta
1 shallot, sliced
½ to 1 jalapeño pepper,* seeded and coarsely chopped
1 clove garlic, sliced
20 large fresh basil leaves
1 tablespoon olive oil
¾ teaspoon salt
⅛ teaspoon black pepper
2 ounces goat cheese *or* ¼ cup ricotta cheese

*Jalapeño peppers can sting and irritate the skin; wear rubber gloves when handling peppers and do not touch eyes. Wash hands after handling.

1. Prepare barbecue grill for direct cooking.

2. Cut tomatoes in half lengthwise; remove seeds. Grill tomatoes, skin sides down, over hot coals about 5 minutes or until skin is blackened and tomatoes are very tender; set aside.

3. Meanwhile, cook pasta according to package directions, omitting salt. Drain; set aside.

4. Combine shallot, jalapeño pepper and garlic in food processor; process until finely chopped. Add tomatoes, basil, oil, salt and black pepper; process until well blended. Return pasta to pan; pour sauce over pasta. Cook 1 minute, stirring frequently.

5. Remove from heat; stir in cheese. Serve immediately.

Makes 4 (1½-cup) servings

Note: Tomatoes can be broiled rather than grilled. Preheat broiler; prepare tomatoes as directed in step 2. Place tomatoes, cut sides down, on broiler pan. Broil tomatoes 5 minutes or until skin is blackened and tomatoes are very tender.

Fire-Roasted Tomatoes with Gemelli Pasta

Grilled Vegetable Fettuccine

1 large zucchini
1 large yellow squash
1 medium red bell pepper
1 medium yellow or green bell pepper
¼ cup non-creamy Italian salad dressing
⅔ cup milk
1 tablespoon margarine or butter
1 (4.7-ounce) package PASTA RONI® Fettuccine Alfredo
¾ cup (3 ounces) crumbled goat cheese or feta cheese
¼ cup julienned fresh basil leaves

1. Preheat grill or broiler. Cut zucchini and squash lengthwise into quarters. Cut bell peppers lengthwise into quarters; discard stems and seeds. Brush dressing over all surfaces of vegetables. Grill over medium coals 10 to 12 minutes or broil on top rack 10 to 12 minutes or until vegetables are tender, turning occasionally.

2. Meanwhile, in medium saucepan, bring 1¼ cups water, milk, margarine, pasta and Special Seasonings to a boil. Reduce heat to medium-low. Gently boil uncovered, 5 to 6 minutes or until pasta is slightly firm, stirring occasionally.

3. Cut grilled vegetables into ½-inch chunks; stir into pasta mixture. Let stand 3 minutes. Top with cheese and basil. *Makes 4 servings*

Tip: Speed up the preparation by using leftover grilled veggies from your weekend barbecue.

Prep Time: 15 minutes
Cook Time: 20 minutes

Grilled Vegetable Fettuccine

Spaghetti Squash with Black Beans and Zucchini

1 spaghetti squash (about 2 pounds)
2 zucchini, cut lengthwise into ¼-inch-thick slices
  Nonstick cooking spray
2 cups chopped seeded tomatoes
1 can (about 15 ounces) black beans, rinsed and drained
2 tablespoons chopped fresh basil
2 tablespoons olive oil
2 tablespoons red wine vinegar
1 large clove garlic, minced
½ teaspoon salt

1. Pierce spaghetti squash in several places with fork. Wrap in large piece of heavy-duty foil, using drugstore wrap technique.* Grill squash on covered grill over medium coals 45 minutes to 1 hour or until easily depressed with back of long-handled spoon, turning a quarter turn every 15 minutes. Remove squash from grill and let stand in foil 10 to 15 minutes.

2. Meanwhile, spray both sides of zucchini slices with cooking spray. Grill on uncovered grill over medium coals 4 minutes or until tender, turning once.

3. Remove spaghetti squash from foil and cut in half; scoop out seeds. With two forks, comb strands of pulp from each half and place in large bowl. Add tomatoes, beans, zucchini and basil. Combine olive oil, vinegar, garlic and salt in small bowl; mix thoroughly. Add to vegetables and toss gently to combine. Serve with grilled French bread and garnish, if desired. *Makes 4 servings*

Place food in the center of an oblong piece of heavy-duty foil, leaving at least a 2-inch border around the food. Bring the two long sides together above the food; fold down in a series of locked folds, allowing room for heat circulation and expansion. Fold short ends up and over again. Press folds firmly to seal the foil packet.

Spaghetti Squash with Black Beans and Zucchini

Grilled Vegetable Muffuletta

10 cloves garlic, peeled
Nonstick cooking spray
1 tablespoon balsamic vinegar
1 tablespoon fresh lemon juice
1 tablespoon olive oil
¼ teaspoon black pepper
1 loaf round whole wheat sourdough bread (1 pound)
1 medium eggplant, cut crosswise into eight ¼-inch-thick slices
2 small yellow squash, cut lengthwise into thin slices
1 small red onion, thinly sliced
1 large red bell pepper, seeded and quartered
2 slices (1 ounce each) Swiss cheese
8 washed spinach leaves

1. Preheat oven to 350°F. Place garlic in ovenproof dish. Spray garlic with cooking spray. Cover with foil; bake 30 to 35 minutes or until garlic is very soft and golden brown.

2. Place garlic, vinegar, lemon juice, olive oil and black pepper in food processor; process, using on-off pulses, until smooth. Set aside.

3. Slice top from bread loaf. Hollow out loaf, leaving ½-inch-thick shell. Reserve bread for another use, if desired.

4. Prepare grill for direct grilling. Brush eggplant, squash, onion and bell pepper with garlic mixture. Arrange vegetables on grid over medium coals. Grill 10 to 12 minutes or until vegetables are crisp-tender, turning once. Separate onion slices into rings.

5. Layer half of eggplant, squash, onion, bell pepper, cheese and spinach in hollowed bread, pressing gently after each layer. Repeat layers with remaining vegetables, cheese and spinach. Replace bread top and serve immediately or cover with plastic wrap and refrigerate up to 4 hours. Cut into wedges before serving.

Makes 6 servings

Grilled Vegetable Muffuletta

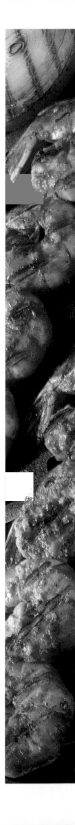

The Seafood Grill

Pineapple Salsa Topped Halibut

Pineapple Salsa
   ¾ cup diced fresh pineapple *or* 1 can (8 ounces) unsweetened
      pineapple chunks, drained
   2 tablespoons finely chopped red bell pepper
   2 tablespoons chopped fresh cilantro
   2 teaspoons vegetable oil
   1 teaspoon minced ginger or finely shredded fresh ginger
   1 teaspoon minced jalapeño pepper or fresh jalapeño pepper*

Halibut
   4 halibut or swordfish steaks (6 ounces each), cut about ¾ inch
      thick
   1 tablespoon garlic-flavored olive oil**
   ¼ teaspoon salt

Jalapeño peppers can sting and irritate the skin; wear rubber gloves when handling peppers and do not touch eyes. Wash hands after handling.

**Or, add ¼ teaspoon minced garlic to 1 tablespoon olive oil.*

1. For salsa, combine pineapple, bell pepper, cilantro, vegetable oil, ginger and jalapeño pepper in small bowl; mix well. Cover; refrigerate until ready to serve.

2. Prepare grill for direct cooking. Brush halibut with olive oil; sprinkle with salt.

3. Grill halibut, on uncovered grill, over medium-hot coals 8 minutes or until halibut flakes when tested with fork, turning once.

4. Top halibut with salsa; serve immediately.   *Makes 4 servings*

Serving Suggestion: Serve with rice pilaf.

Pineapple Salsa Topped Halibut

Sizzling Florida Shrimp

1½ pounds Florida Shrimp, peeled and deveined
1 cup Florida mushrooms, cut into halves
½ cup Florida red bell pepper pieces (1-inch pieces)
½ cup Florida onion pieces (1-inch pieces)
1 (8.9-ounce) jar Flavor Medleys™ Lemon Pepper Sauce

Arrange shrimp on wooden skewers with mushrooms, red bell pepper and onion. Place skewers in glass dish and cover with sauce, reserving about 2 tablespoons for basting during cooking. Cover and refrigerate for 1 hour. Prepare grill surface by cleaning and coating with oil. Coals are ready when coals are no longer flaming but are covered with gray ash. Place skewers on grill about 6 inches from coals. Grill shrimp for 3 to 4 minutes on each side, basting before turning once. Serve with sautéed asparagus and grilled garlic bread. *Makes 4 servings*

Favorite recipe from **Florida Department of Agriculture and Consumer Services, Bureau of Seafood and Aquaculture**

Barbecued Salmon

4 salmon steaks, ¾ to 1 inch thick
3 tablespoons lemon juice
2 tablespoons soy sauce
Salt and black pepper
½ cup KC MASTERPIECE™ Original Barbecue Sauce
Fresh oregano sprigs
Grilled mushrooms (optional)

Rinse salmon; pat dry with paper towels. Combine lemon juice and soy sauce in shallow glass dish. Add salmon; let stand at cool room temperature no more than 15 to 20 minutes, turning salmon several times. Remove salmon from marinade; discard marinade. Season lightly with salt and pepper.

Lightly oil hot grid to prevent sticking. Grill salmon on covered grill over medium KINGSFORD® Briquets 10 to 14 minutes. Halfway through cooking time brush salmon with barbecue sauce, then turn and continue grilling until fish flakes when tested with fork. Remove fish from grill; brush with remaining barbecue sauce. Garnish with oregano sprigs and mushrooms. *Makes 4 servings*

Sizzling Florida Shrimp

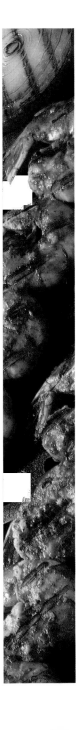

Seafood Tacos with Fruit Salsa

        2 tablespoons lemon juice
        1 teaspoon chili powder
        1 teaspoon ground allspice
        1 teaspoon olive oil
        1 teaspoon minced garlic
        1 to 2 teaspoons grated lemon peel
      ½ teaspoon ground cloves
        1 pound halibut or snapper fillets
      12 (6-inch) corn tortillas *or* 6 (7- to 8-inch) flour tortillas
        3 cups shredded romaine lettuce
        1 small red onion, halved and thinly sliced
        Fruit Salsa (recipe follows)

1. Combine lemon juice, chili powder, allspice, oil, garlic, lemon peel and cloves in small bowl. Rub fish with spice mixture; cover and refrigerate while grill heats. (Fish may be cut into smaller pieces for easier handling.)

2. Prepare Fruit Salsa. Spray grid with nonstick cooking spray. Adjust grid 4 to 6 inches above heat. Preheat grill to medium-high heat. Grill fish, covered, 3 minutes or until fish is lightly browned on bottom. Carefully turn fish over; grill 2 minutes or until fish is opaque in center. Remove from heat and cut into 12 pieces, removing bones if necessary. Cover to keep warm.

3. Place tortillas on grill in single layer and heat 5 to 10 seconds; turn and cook 5 to 10 seconds or until hot and pliable. Stack; cover to keep warm.

4. Top each tortilla with ¼ cup lettuce, red onion, fish and Fruit Salsa.

Makes 6 servings

Fruit Salsa

        1 small ripe papaya, peeled, seeded and diced
        1 firm small banana, diced
        2 green onions, minced
        3 tablespoons chopped fresh cilantro or mint
        3 tablespoons lime juice
        2 jalapeño peppers, seeded and minced

Combine all ingredients in small bowl. Serve at room temperature.

Seafood Tacos with Fruit Salsa

Grilled Swordfish with Hot Red Sauce

2 to 3 green onions
4 swordfish or halibut steaks (about 1½ pounds total)
2 tablespoons hot bean paste*
2 tablespoons soy sauce
2 tablespoons Sesame Salt (recipe follows)
4 teaspoons sugar
4 cloves garlic, minced
1 tablespoon dark sesame oil
⅛ teaspoon black pepper

*Available in specialty stores or Asian markets.

1. Spray grid of grill or broiler rack with nonstick cooking spray. Prepare coals for grilling or preheat broiler.

2. Cut off and discard root ends of green onions. Finely chop enough green onions to measure ¼ cup; set aside. Prepare Sesame Salt; set aside.

3. Rinse swordfish and pat dry with paper towels. Place in shallow glass dish.

4. Combine green onions, hot bean paste, soy sauce, Sesame Salt, sugar, garlic, sesame oil and pepper in small bowl; mix well.

5. Spread half of marinade over fish; turn fish over and spread with remaining marinade. Cover with plastic wrap and refrigerate 30 minutes.

6. Remove fish from marinade; discard remaining marinade. Place fish on prepared grid. Grill fish over medium-hot coals or broil 4 to 5 minutes per side or until fish is opaque. Garnish as desired. *Makes 4 servings*

Sesame Salt

½ cup sesame seeds
¼ teaspoon salt

Heat small skillet over medium heat. Add sesame seeds; cook and stir about 5 minutes or until seeds are golden. Cool. Crush toasted sesame seeds and salt with mortar and pestle or process in clean coffee or spice grinder. Refrigerate in covered glass jar.

Grilled Swordfish with Hot Red Sauce

Easy Salmon Burgers with Honey Barbecue Sauce

⅓ **cup honey**
⅓ **cup ketchup**
1½ **teaspoons cider vinegar**
1 **teaspoon prepared horseradish**
¼ **teaspoon minced garlic**
⅛ **teaspoon crushed red pepper flakes (optional)**
1 **can (7½ ounces) salmon, drained**
½ **cup dried bread crumbs**
¼ **cup chopped onion**
3 **tablespoons chopped green bell pepper**
1 **egg white**
2 **hamburger buns, toasted**

In small bowl, combine honey, ketchup, vinegar, horseradish, garlic and red pepper flakes until well blended. Set aside half of sauce. In separate bowl, mix together salmon, bread crumbs, onion, green pepper and egg white. Blend in 2 tablespoons remaining sauce. Divide salmon mixture into 2 patties, ½ to ¾ inch thick. Place patties on well-oiled grill, 4 to 6 inches from hot coals. Grill, turning 2 to 3 times and baste with remaining sauce, until burgers are browned and cooked through. Or place patties on lightly greased baking sheet. Broil 4 to 6 inches from heat source, turning 2 to 3 times and basting with remaining sauce, until cooked through. Place on hamburger buns and serve with reserved sauce. *Makes 2 servings*

Favorite recipe from **National Honey Board**

Easy Salmon Burgers with Honey Barbecue Sauce

Grilled Tequila Lime Shrimp

1 pound large uncooked shrimp, peeled and deveined
½ yellow bell pepper, cut into ½-inch pieces
6 green onions, sliced into 1½-inch pieces
16 cherry or pear tomatoes
8 wooden skewers
1 cup LAWRY'S® Tequila Lime Marinade With Lime Juice
1 lime, sliced into 8 wedges

Thread shrimp, pepper, onions and tomatoes onto skewers, dividing ingredients equally. Brush heavily and frequently with Tequila Lime Marinade while grilling. Cook until shrimp just turn pink; do not overcook. Serve each skewer with wedge of lime.

Makes 8 skewers (4 servings)

Meal Idea: Serve with your favorite pasta, rice or orzo side dish.

Variations: Also great served in pita bread with shredded lettuce and lime juice squeezed over the top. Or serve wrapped up in a flour tortilla as a wrap sandwich. Both ideas are great for picnics and parties!

Hint: Soak wooden skewers in water for at least 30 minutes before using to prevent burning.

Prep Time: 15 minutes
Cook Time: 7 to 10 minutes

Grilled Tequila Lime Shrimp

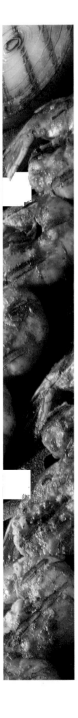

Catfish with Fresh Corn Relish

4 catfish fillets (each about 6 ounces and at least ½ inch thick)
2 tablespoons paprika
½ teaspoon ground red pepper
½ teaspoon salt
   Fresh Corn Relish (recipe follows)
   Lime wedges
   Grilled baking potatoes (optional)
   Tarragon sprigs for garnish

Rinse fish; pat dry with paper towels. Combine paprika, red pepper and salt in cup; lightly sprinkle on both sides of fish.

Oil hot grid to help prevent sticking. Grill fish, on a covered grill, over medium KINGSFORD® Briquets, 5 to 9 minutes. Halfway through cooking time, turn fish over and continue grilling until fish turns from translucent to opaque throughout. (Grilling time depends on the thickness of fish; allow 3 to 5 minutes for each ½ inch of thickness.) Serve with Fresh Corn Relish, lime wedges and potatoes, if desired. Garnish with tarragon sprigs.   *Makes 4 servings*

Fresh Corn Relish

¼ cup cooked fresh corn or thawed frozen corn
¼ cup finely diced green bell pepper
¼ cup finely slivered red onion
 1 tablespoon vegetable oil
 2 tablespoons seasoned (sweet) rice vinegar
   Salt and black pepper
½ cup cherry tomatoes, cut into quarters

Toss together corn, green pepper, onion, oil and vinegar in medium bowl. Season with salt and pepper. Cover and refrigerate until ready to serve. Just before serving, gently mix in tomatoes.   *Makes about 1½ cups*

Catfish with Fresh Corn Relish

Tuna Vera Cruz

3 tablespoons tequila, rum or vodka
2 tablespoons lime juice
2 teaspoons grated lime peel
1 piece (1-inch cube) fresh ginger, minced
2 cloves garlic, minced
1 teaspoon salt
1 teaspoon sugar
½ teaspoon ground cumin
¼ teaspoon ground cinnamon
¼ teaspoon black pepper
1 tablespoon vegetable oil
1½ pounds fresh tuna, halibut, swordfish or shark steaks
Lemon and lime wedges
Fresh rosemary sprigs

Combine tequila, lime juice, lime peel, ginger, garlic, salt, sugar, cumin, cinnamon and pepper in 2-quart glass dish; stir in oil. Add tuna; turn to coat. Cover and refrigerate at least 30 minutes. Remove tuna from marinade; discard marinade. Grill tuna over medium-hot KINGSFORD® Briquets about 4 minutes per side until fish flakes when tested with fork. Garnish with lemon wedges, lime wedges and rosemary sprigs. *Makes 4 servings*

The most popular variety of barbecue sauce is hickory flavored.

Tuna Vera Cruz

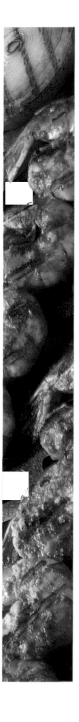

Teriyaki Grilled Snapper

**2 whole red snappers or striped bass (1½ pounds each), scaled and
        gutted**
⅓ cup *French's*® Worcestershire Sauce
⅓ cup peanut oil
⅓ cup rice vinegar
¼ cup chopped green onion
1 tablespoon dark sesame oil
1 tablespoon chopped peeled fresh ginger
3 cloves garlic, chopped
   Asian Slaw (recipe follows)

Rinse fish and place in large resealable plastic food storage bag or shallow glass
dish. To prepare marinade, place Worcestershire, peanut oil, vinegar, onion, sesame
oil, ginger and garlic in food processor or blender. Cover and process until well
blended. Reserve ¼ cup marinade for serving. Pour remaining marinade over fish.
Seal bag or cover dish and marinate in refrigerator 1 hour.

Place fish in oiled grilling basket, reserving marinade for basting. Grill over medium-
high coals 10 to 12 minutes per side or until fish flakes when tested with fork, basting
occasionally with basting marinade. (Do not baste during last 5 minutes of cooking.)
Discard remaining basting marinade. Carefully remove bones from fish. Pour reserved
¼ cup marinade over fish. Serve with Asian Slaw. Garnish as desired.

Makes 4 servings

Prep Time: 10 minutes
Marinate Time: 1 hour
Cook Time: 25 minutes

Asian Slaw

½ small head napa cabbage, shredded (about 4 cups)*
3 carrots
2 red or yellow bell peppers, seeded and cut into very thin strips
¼ pound snow peas, trimmed and cut into thin strips
⅓ cup peanut oil
¼ cup rice vinegar
3 tablespoons *French's*® Worcestershire Sauce
1 tablespoon dark sesame oil
1 tablespoon honey
2 cloves garlic, minced

You can substitute 4 cups shredded green cabbage for the napa cabbage.

Place vegetables in large bowl. Whisk together peanut oil, vinegar, Worcestershire, sesame oil, honey and garlic in small bowl until well blended. Pour dressing over vegetables; toss well to coat evenly. Cover and refrigerate 1 hour before serving.

Makes 4 to 6 servings

Prep Time: 20 minutes
Chill Time: 1 hour

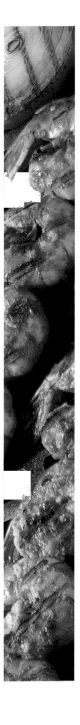

Mesquite-Grilled Salmon Fillets

2 tablespoons olive oil
1 clove garlic, minced
2 tablespoons lemon juice
1 teaspoon grated lemon peel
½ teaspoon dried dill weed
½ teaspoon dried thyme leaves
¼ teaspoon salt
¼ teaspoon black pepper
4 salmon fillets, ¾ to 1 inch thick (about 5 ounces each)

1. Cover 1 cup mesquite chips with cold water; soak 20 to 30 minutes. Spray grid with nonstick cooking spray. Prepare grill for direct cooking.

2. Combine oil and garlic in small microwavable bowl. Microwave at HIGH 1 minute or until garlic is tender. Add lemon juice, lemon peel, dill, thyme, salt and pepper; whisk until blended. Brush skinless sides of salmon with half of lemon mixture.

3. Drain mesquite chips; sprinkle chips over coals. Place salmon, skin side up, on grid. Grill, covered, over medium-high heat 4 to 5 minutes; turn and brush with remaining lemon mixture. Grill 4 to 5 minutes or until salmon flakes when tested with fork. *Makes 4 servings*

Honey-Dijon Grilled Shrimp

¼ cup lemon juice
¼ cup orange juice
¼ cup honey
2 tablespoons Dijon-style mustard
½ teaspoon salt
¼ teaspoon white pepper
1 pound raw large shrimp, peeled and deveined
1 onion, cut into wedges
8 cherry tomatoes
2 limes, cut into wedges

Combine lemon juice, orange juice, honey, mustard, salt and pepper in medium bowl; mix well. Arrange shrimp, onion, tomatoes and limes in well-oiled wire grill basket; brush with marinade mixture. Grill 4 to 6 minutes or until shrimp are pink, turning once and basting often with marinade mixture. *Makes 4 servings*

Mesquite-Grilled Salmon Fillet

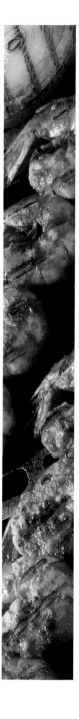

Grilled Red Snapper with Avocado-Papaya Salsa

1 teaspoon ground coriander seeds
1 teaspoon paprika
¾ teaspoon salt
⅛ to ¼ teaspoon ground red pepper
1 tablespoon olive oil
4 skinless red snapper or halibut fish fillets (5 to 7 ounces each)
½ cup diced ripe avocado
½ cup diced ripe papaya
2 tablespoons chopped fresh cilantro
1 tablespoon fresh lime juice
4 lime wedges

1. Prepare grill for direct grilling. Combine coriander, paprika, salt and red pepper in small bowl or cup; mix well.

2. Brush oil over fish. Sprinkle 2½ teaspoons spice mixture over fish; set aside remaining spice mixture. Place fish on oiled grid over medium-hot heat. Grill 5 minutes per side or until fish is opaque.

3. Meanwhile, combine avocado, papaya, cilantro, lime juice and remaining spice mixture in medium bowl; mix well. Serve fish with salsa and garnish with lime wedges.
Makes 4 servings

Grilled Red Snapper with Avocado-Papaya Salsa

Grilled Salmon Quesadillas with Cucumber Salsa

1 medium cucumber, peeled, seeded and finely chopped
½ cup green or red salsa
1 (8-ounce) salmon fillet
3 tablespoons olive oil, divided
4 (10-inch) flour tortillas, warmed
6 ounces goat cheese, crumbled or 1½ cups (6 ounces) shredded Monterey Jack cheese
¼ cup drained sliced pickled jalapeño peppers*

*Jalapeño peppers can sting and irritate the skin; wear rubber gloves when handling peppers and do not touch eyes. Wash hands after handling.

1. Prepare grill for direct cooking. Combine cucumber and salsa in small bowl; set aside.

2. Brush salmon with 2 tablespoons oil. Grill, covered, over medium-hot coals 5 to 6 minutes per side or until fish flakes when tested with fork. Transfer to plate; flake with fork.

3. Spoon salmon evenly over half of each tortilla, leaving 1-inch border. Sprinkle with cheese and jalapeño pepper slices. Fold tortillas in half. Brush tortillas with remaining 1 tablespoon oil.

4. Grill quesadillas over medium-hot coals until browned on both sides and cheese is melted. Serve with Cucumber Salsa. *Makes 4 servings*

Prep and Cook Time: 20 minutes

Grilled Salmon Quesadilla with Cucumber Salsa

Salmon with Fresh Pineapple Salsa

1 bottle (12 ounces) LAWRY'S® Teriyaki Marinade with Pineapple Juice, divided
1¼ pounds fresh salmon fillet *or* steaks
1 cup diced fresh or canned pineapple (½-inch pieces), well-drained
¼ cup diced red onion (¼-inch pieces)
1 tablespoon chopped fresh cilantro
2 tablespoons diced red bell pepper (¼-inch pieces)
1 tablespoon minced fresh jalapeño chile

In large resealable plastic bag, combine 1 cup Teriyaki Marinade and salmon; seal bag. Marinate in refrigerator for 30 minutes or up to several hours. In small bowl, lightly mix together 2 tablespoons Marinade, pineapple, onion, cilantro, red bell pepper and chile. Let pineapple salsa stand at room temperature up to 1 hour. Remove salmon from bag, discarding used marinade. Grill salmon on both sides over high heat for 5 to 6 minutes per side, brushing with remaining Marinade, until fish begins to flake. Cut fish into 4 pieces; serve with room temperature salsa on top or on the side. *Makes 4 servings*

Meal Idea: Serve with your favorite pasta, rice or orzo as a side dish. Also great served as a wrap in a large flour tortilla. Simply break-up salmon into chunks, top with salsa and roll up to enclose filling.

Variations: Also great with LAWRY'S® Caribbean Jerk Marinade with Papaya Juice *or* LAWRY'S® Hawaiian Marinade with Tropical Fruit Juices instead of Teriyaki Marinade.

Prep Time: 15 minutes
Marinate Time: 30 minutes
Cook Time: 10 to 12 minutes

Salmon with Fresh Pineapple Salsa

Shanghai Fish Packets

4 orange roughy or tilefish fillets (4 to 6 ounces each)
¼ cup mirin* or Rhine wine
3 tablespoons soy sauce
1 tablespoon dark sesame oil
1½ teaspoons grated fresh ginger
¼ teaspoon red pepper flakes
1 tablespoon peanut or vegetable oil
1 clove garlic, minced
1 package (10 ounces) fresh spinach leaves, destemmed

*Mirin is a Japanese sweet wine available in Japanese markets and the gourmet section of large supermarkets.

1. Prepare grill for direct cooking.

2. Place orange roughy in single layer in large shallow dish. Combine mirin, soy sauce, sesame oil, ginger and red pepper flakes in small bowl; pour over orange roughy. Cover; marinate in refrigerator 20 minutes.

3. Heat peanut oil in large skillet over medium heat. Add garlic; cook and stir 1 minute. Add spinach; cook and stir until wilted, about 3 minutes, tossing with 2 wooden spoons.

4. Place spinach mixture in center of four 12-inch squares of heavy-duty foil. Remove orange roughy from marinade; reserve marinade. Place 1 orange roughy fillet over each mound of spinach. Drizzle reserved marinade evenly over orange roughy. Wrap in foil.

5. Place packets on grid. Grill packets, on covered grill, over medium coals 15 to 18 minutes or until orange roughy flakes when tested with fork.

Makes 4 servings

Shanghai Fish Packet

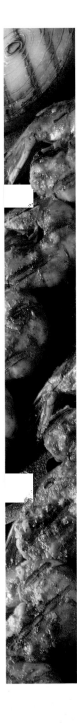

Skewered Tuna Niçoise

½ cup olive oil
¼ cup balsamic vinegar
3 cloves garlic, chopped
1 tablespoon chopped fresh rosemary
½ teaspoon black pepper
1 pound tuna steaks, cut into 1½-inch chunks
1½ pounds medium red potatoes, quartered
1 large red onion, cut into 8 equal wedges
½ pound green beans, trimmed and cut into 2-inch lengths
8 cups mixed lettuce
1 large tomato, cut into 8 wedges
12 ripe olives, quartered
2 hard-cooked egg whites, slivered
1 tablespoon drained capers

1. Combine oil, vinegar, garlic, rosemary and pepper in food processor or blender; process until rosemary is finely minced. Place ¼ cup dressing in medium bowl. Add tuna; turn to coat. Cover and refrigerate up to 1 hour. Pour remaining dressing into jar with tight-fitting lid.

2. Cook potatoes in boiling water 6 minutes or until just tender. Transfer to medium bowl; add onion. Shake dressing and pour about 2 tablespoons over potato mixture; toss gently to coat.

3. Add green beans to simmering water; cook 3 minutes or until crisp-tender. Drain and rinse under cold water.

4. Thread potatoes and onion onto skewers. Thread tuna onto separate skewers. Grill vegetables over medium-hot coals about 10 minutes or until well browned. Grill tuna 6 to 8 minutes or until fish flakes when tested with fork.

5. Toss lettuce with ¼ cup dressing; transfer to large platter. Toss green beans with remaining dressing; arrange over lettuce. Remove tuna, potatoes and onion from skewers; place on salad. Garnish with tomato, olives, egg whites and capers.

Makes 6 servings

Skewered Tuna Niçoise

Seafood Kabobs

Nonstick cooking spray
1 pound uncooked large shrimp, peeled and deveined
10 ounces skinless swordfish or halibut steaks, cut 1 inch thick
2 tablespoons honey mustard
2 teaspoons fresh lemon juice
8 slices bacon (regular slice, not thick)
Lemon wedges and fresh herbs (optional)

1. Spray grid with nonstick cooking spray. Prepare grill for direct cooking.

2. Place shrimp in shallow glass dish. Cut swordfish into 1-inch cubes; add to dish. Combine mustard and lemon juice in small bowl. Pour over shrimp mixture; toss lightly to coat.

3. Pierce one 12-inch metal skewer through 1 end of bacon slice. Add 1 piece shrimp. Pierce skewer through bacon slice again, wrapping bacon slice around 1 side of shrimp.

4. Add 1 piece swordfish. Pierce bacon slice again, wrapping bacon around opposite side of swordfish. Continue adding seafood and wrapping with bacon, pushing ingredients to middle of skewer until end of bacon slice is reached. Repeat with 7 more skewers. Brush any remaining mustard mixture over skewers.

5. Place skewers on grid. Grill, covered, over medium heat 8 to 10 minutes or until shrimp are opaque and swordfish flakes when tested with fork, turning halfway through grilling time. Garnish with lemon wedges and fresh herbs, if desired.

Makes 4 servings (2 kabobs per serving)

Note: Kabobs can be prepared up to 3 hours before grilling. Cover and refrigerate until ready to grill.

Seafood Kabobs

Grill Go-Withs

Grilled Peaches with Raspberry Sauce

      1 package (10 ounces) frozen raspberries, thawed
 1½ teaspoons lemon juice
      3 tablespoons brown sugar
      1 tablespoon rum (optional)
      1 teaspoon ground cinnamon
      4 medium peaches, peeled, halved and pitted
      2 teaspoons butter
         Fresh mint sprigs (optional)

1. Combine raspberries and lemon juice in food processor fitted with metal blade; process until smooth. Refrigerate until ready to serve.

2. Combine brown sugar, rum, if desired, and cinnamon in medium bowl; coat peach halves with mixture. Place peach halves, cut sides up, on foil. Dot with butter. Fold foil over peaches, leaving head space for heat circulation; seal foil. Grill over medium coals for 15 minutes.

3. To serve, spoon 2 tablespoons raspberry sauce over each peach half. Garnish with fresh mint sprig, if desired. *Makes 4 servings*

ABC Slaw

      2 green apples, cored and cut into thin strips
      1 package (10 ounces) broccoli slaw with carrots
      3 stalks celery, trimmed and cut into thin diagonal slices
      1 bulb fennel, trimmed and cut into thin strips
      4 tablespoons creamy salad dressing
      1 tablespoon lemon juice
 ½ teaspoon red pepper flakes

Combine all ingredients in bowl; mix well. Chill 1 hour before serving.
Makes 4 to 6 servings

Grilled Peach with Raspberry Sauce

Shiner Bock BBQ Bean Salad

⅓ cup prepared spicy barbecue sauce
¼ cup bock beer
3 tablespoons cider vinegar
1 tablespoon molasses
1 teaspoon hot sauce, or to taste
½ teaspoon mustard seeds
1 can (15½ ounces) pinto beans, rinsed and drained
4 ribs celery, halved and sliced
3 plum tomatoes, seeded and coarsely chopped
1 bunch green onions, trimmed and chopped
Salt and pepper

Whisk together barbecue sauce, beer, vinegar, molasses, hot sauce and mustard seeds in large bowl. Add beans, celery, tomatoes and green onions; toss to coat. Season with salt, pepper and hot sauce. (Salad will keep, covered, in refrigerator for up to 2 days. Bring to room temperature before serving.)   *Makes 4 to 6 servings*

Ambrosia

1 can (20 ounces) DOLE® Pineapple Chunks
1 can (11 or 15 ounces) DOLE® Mandarin Oranges
1 firm, large DOLE® Banana, sliced (optional)
1½ cups DOLE® Seedless Grapes
1 cup miniature marshmallows
1 cup flaked coconut
½ cup pecan halves or coarsely chopped nuts
1 cup vanilla yogurt or sour cream
1 tablespoon brown sugar

● Drain pineapple chunks and mandarin oranges. In large bowl, combine pineapple chunks, mandarin oranges, banana, grapes, marshmallows, coconut and nuts. In 1-quart measure, combine yogurt and brown sugar. Stir into fruit mixture. Refrigerate, covered, 1 hour or overnight.   *Makes 4 servings*

Shiner Bock BBQ Bean Salad

Mango Batido

1 large mango
1¾ cups fat-free (skim) milk
2 tablespoons frozen orange-peach-mango juice concentrate
4 ice cubes
⅛ teaspoon almond extract (optional)

1. Peel mango. Cut fruit away from pit; cut fruit into cubes.

2. Combine all ingredients in blender; blend until smooth. Serve immediately.

Makes 4 servings

Tip: Chill mango before preparing recipe or use frozen mango chunks.

Fire-Roasted Corn and Cherry Salsa

1 cup dried tart cherries
½ cup water
3 fresh ears of corn, shucked
½ cup lemon or lime juice
½ cup chopped red onion
¼ cup cilantro, chopped
2 to 3 whole chipotle chilies in adobo sauce, finely chopped
1 tablespoon finely chopped garlic
Salt to taste

1. Heat cherries and water in small saucepan. Simmer about 5 minutes or until cherries have plumped and water is slightly syrupy. Set aside to cool.

2. Meanwhile, roast each ear of corn directly over gas flame on stovetop or over gas grill (similar to roasting peppers). Turn until each ear is slightly charred all around. Set aside to cool. Cut corn kernels from cobs.

3. Combine corn, cherries with liquid, lemon juice, onion, cilantro, chilies and garlic. Season with salt to taste.   *Makes 2 cups or 6 (½-cup) servings*

Note: This makes a medium-hot salsa. Use fewer or more chipotle chilies to make salsa milder or hotter.

Serving suggestions: Serve with grilled chicken, pork or fish.

Favorite recipe from **Cherry Marketing Institute**

Mango Batido

Best 'Cue Coleslaw

⅓ **cup vegetable oil**
⅓ **cup dill pickle relish**
 3 tablespoons lime juice
 2 tablespoons honey
 1 teaspoon salt
 1 teaspoon ground cumin
 1 teaspoon ground red pepper
 1 teaspoon black pepper
 1 small head green cabbage, rinsed and very thinly sliced
 2 large carrots, shredded
 1 bunch green onions, sliced
 5 radishes, sliced

Whisk together oil, relish, lime juice, honey, salt, cumin, ground red pepper and black pepper in large bowl. Add cabbage, carrots, green onions and radishes; stir until well combined. Chill at least 1 hour before serving.

Makes 6 to 8 servings

Texas Tip: Try adding slivered apples instead of the dill pickles for a sweet taste.

Best 'Cue Coleslaw

Grilled Banana Split

1 large ripe firm banana
½ teaspoon melted butter
2 tablespoons chocolate syrup
½ teaspoon orange liqueur (optional)
⅔ cup vanilla ice cream
2 tablespoons toasted sliced almonds

1. Prepare grill for direct cooking.

2. Cut unpeeled banana lengthwise; brush melted butter over cut sides. Grill banana, cut sides down, over medium-hot coals 2 minutes or until lightly browned; turn. Grill 2 minutes or until tender. Combine chocolate syrup and liqueur, if desired, in small bowl.

3. Cut banana halves in half crosswise; carefully remove peel. Place 2 pieces banana in each bowl; top with ⅓ cup ice cream, 1 tablespoon chocolate syrup and 1 tablespoon almonds. Serve immediately. *Makes 2 servings*

Spanish Rice with Avocado

1 tablespoon butter or margarine
1 tablespoon olive oil
1 small onion, finely chopped
1 clove garlic, minced
1 cup uncooked rice
¼ teaspoon salt
¼ teaspoon dried oregano leaves
¼ teaspoon ground cumin
¼ teaspoon ground turmeric
1 can (14½ ounces) chicken broth
1 small avocado

Heat butter and oil in 2-quart pan over medium heat. When butter is melted, add onion and garlic; cook until onion is tender. Add rice; cook, stirring constantly, 3 minutes or until rice looks milky and opaque. Add salt, oregano, cumin, turmeric and chicken broth; bring to a boil. Cover; reduce heat and simmer 20 to 25 minutes or until rice is tender and all liquid is absorbed. Peel and pit avocado; dice. Fluff rice with fork; add avocado and toss gently. Turn off heat; let stand 5 minutes before serving. *Makes 4 to 6 servings*

Grilled Banana Split

Basil Biscuits

2 cups all-purpose flour
4 tablespoons grated Parmesan cheese, divided
1 tablespoon baking powder
½ teaspoon baking soda
¼ teaspoon salt (optional)
4 tablespoons Neufchâtel cheese
2 tablespoons butter, divided
6 ounces plain nonfat yogurt
⅓ cup slivered fresh basil leaves

1. Combine flour, 2 tablespoons Parmesan, baking powder, baking soda and salt, if desired, in large bowl. Cut in Neufchâtel and 1 tablespoon butter with pastry blender or two knives until mixture forms coarse crumbs. Stir in yogurt and basil, mixing just until dough clings together. Turn dough out onto lightly floured surface and gently pat into ball. Knead just until dough holds together. Pat and roll dough into 7-inch log. Cut into 7 (1-inch-thick) slices.

2. Spray 10-inch cast iron skillet or Dutch oven with nonstick cooking spray; arrange biscuits in skillet. Melt remaining 1 tablespoon butter and brush over biscuit tops. Sprinkle with remaining 2 tablespoons Parmesan. Place skillet on grid set 4 to 6 inches above medium-hot coals (about 375°F); cover grill. Bake 20 to 40 minutes or until golden and firm on top. *Makes 7 biscuits*

Note: To prepare a charcoal grill for baking, arrange a single, solid, even layer of medium coals in bottom of charcoal grill. If necessary, reduce temperature by either allowing coals to cook down or removing 3 or 4 coals at a time to a fireproof container until desired temperature is reached. For a gas grill, begin on medium heat and adjust heat as necessary. Besides raising or lowering the temperature setting, you can turn off one side of the grill or set each side to a different temperature.

Basil Biscuits

Orange Iced Tea

2 SUNKIST® oranges
4 cups boiling water
5 tea bags
  Ice cubes
  Honey or brown sugar to taste

With vegetable peeler, peel each orange in continuous spiral, removing only outer colored layer of peel (eat peeled fruit or save for other uses). In large pitcher, pour boiling water over tea bags and orange peel. Cover and steep 5 minutes. Remove tea bags; chill tea mixture with peel in covered container. To serve, remove peel and pour over ice cubes in tall glasses. Sweeten to taste with honey. Garnish with orange quarter-cartwheel slices and fresh mint leaves, if desired.

Makes 4 (8-ounce) servings

Lemon Herbal Iced Tea

2 SUNKIST® lemons
4 cups boiling water
6 herbal tea bags (peppermint and spearmint blend or
    ginger-flavored)
  Ice cubes
  Honey or sugar to taste

With vegetable peeler, peel each lemon in continuous spiral, removing only outer colored layer of peel (save peeled fruit for other uses). In large pitcher, pour boiling water over tea bags and lemon peel. Cover and steep 10 minutes. Remove tea bags; chill tea mixture with peel in covered container. To serve, remove peel and pour over ice cubes in tall glasses. Sweeten to taste with honey. Garnish with lemon half-cartwheel slices, if desired.

Makes 4 (8-ounce) servings

Orange Iced Tea and Lemon Herbal Iced Tea

Sweet & Tangy Marinated Vegetables

8 cups mixed fresh vegetables, such as broccoli, cauliflower, zucchini, carrots and red bell peppers, cut into 1 to 1½-inch pieces
⅓ cup distilled white vinegar
¼ cup sugar
¼ cup water
1 packet (1 ounce) HIDDEN VALLEY® The Original Ranch® Salad Dressing & Seasoning Mix

Place vegetables in a gallon size Glad® Zipper Storage Bag. Whisk together vinegar, sugar, water and salad dressing & seasoning mix until sugar dissolves; pour over vegetables. Seal bag and shake to coat. Refrigerate 4 hours or overnight, turning bag occasionally. *Makes 8 servings*

Note: Vegetables will keep up to 3 days in refrigerator.

Honey-Dijon Fresh Fruit Chutney

1 cup coarsely chopped fruit, such as mango, peaches, pineapple and kiwifruit
½ cup unsweetened applesauce
½ cup chopped celery
5 tablespoons honey
¼ cup finely chopped red onion
3 tablespoons Dijon mustard
2 tablespoons chopped fresh mint or cilantro
1 tablespoon lime or lemon juice
2 teaspoons grated fresh gingerroot
Crushed red pepper flakes to taste
Salt to taste

Combine all ingredients in medium bowl; stir until well blended. Chill until ready to serve. Serve with sliced grilled turkey or pork tenderloin. Also a great relish on sandwiches. *Makes about 2 cups*

*Favorite recipe from **National Honey Board***

Sweet & Tangy Marinated Vegetables

Pineapple Boats with Citrus Creme

1 large DOLE® Fresh Pineapple
1 DOLE® Banana, peeled, sliced
1 orange, peeled, sliced
1 apple, cored, sliced
1 DOLE® Pear, cored, sliced
1 cup seedless DOLE® Grapes (red and green)

Citrus Creme
1 cup plain nonfat yogurt
2 tablespoons brown sugar
1 tablespoon minced crystallized ginger (optional)
1 teaspoon grated orange peel
1 teaspoon grated lime peel

• Cut pineapple in half lengthwise through the crown. Cut fruit from shells, leaving shells intact. Core and chunk fruit.

• Combine pineapple chunks with remaining fruit. Spoon into pineapple boats.

• Combine all ingredients for Citrus Creme. Serve with pineapple boats.

Makes 8 servings

Prep Time: 20 minutes

Why is it that no matter how you position a grill the smoke always blows towards you?

Pineapple Boat with Citrus Creme

Smoked New Potato Salad

2 cups hardwood chips
Dill Vinaigrette (recipe follows)
2 pounds new potatoes
1 medium yellow or red bell pepper, halved
1 tablespoon olive oil
2 tablespoons (1 ounce) crumbled feta cheese

1. Cover hardwood chips with water and soak for at least 30 minutes. (If using wooden or bamboo skewers, soak in water 20 to 30 minutes to prevent from burning.) Prepare Dill Vinaigrette; set aside.

2. Place potatoes in large saucepan and cover with water; bring to a boil over high heat. Reduce heat to medium and simmer 8 to 10 minutes or until crisp-tender; drain and cool. (Potatoes can be prepared ahead and refrigerated for up to 1 day.)

3. Grill bell pepper halves skin sides down on covered grill over medium coals 15 to 25 minutes or until skin is charred, without turning. Remove from grill and place in plastic bag until cool enough to handle, about 10 minutes; remove pepper skin with paring knife and discard. Chop pepper; set aside.

4. Cut potatoes into halves and place in medium bowl. Drizzle with oil; stir to coat potatoes evenly. Spray hinged wire grill basket with nonstick cooking spray. Place potatoes in basket, arranging in single layer; close securely. (Or, thread potatoes onto 5 or 6 prepared skewers.) Drain hardwood chips and sprinkle over hot coals. Grill potatoes on covered grill over medium to hot coals 12 to 16 minutes (6 to 10 minutes if using skewers) or until golden, turning once. Remove to serving bowl; add bell pepper and gently stir in dressing. Sprinkle with cheese; mix gently. Garnish as desired.

Makes 6 servings

Dill Vinaigrette

¼ cup thinly sliced green onions
2 tablespoons chopped fresh dill weed
2 tablespoons rice vinegar or cider vinegar
1 tablespoon Dijon mustard
1 tablespoon olive oil

Whisk all ingredients together in small bowl.

Smoked New Potato Salad

Brandied Fruit

2 **large ripe mangos, papayas or peaches**
2 **to 3 large ripe plums, halved and pitted**
24 **sweet cherries, halved and pitted**
6 **tablespoons sugar**
¼ **cup brandy**
2 **tablespoons chopped crystallized ginger**
1 **tablespoon fresh lemon juice**
2 **teaspoons cornstarch**
1 **tablespoon orange- or cherry-flavored liqueur (optional)**
Angel food cake (optional)

1. Spray grillproof 9-inch square baking pan or pie plate with nonstick cooking spray; set aside. Peel mangos; slice pulp from pit and cut into ½-inch-wide slices. Place in prepared baking pan. Cut each plum half into 4 wedges; add to pan. Stir in cherries.

2. Combine sugar, brandy, ginger, lemon juice and cornstarch in small bowl; stir until cornstarch dissolves and pour over fruit. Cover tightly with foil.

3. Place pan on grid. Grill on covered grill over low to medium coals 20 to 30 minutes or until juices simmer and fruit is tender; stir in liqueur, if desired. Spoon over angel food cake, if desired, or serve in small bowls.

Makes 6 servings

Tip: Firm fruits hold up best on the grill. Consider stirring in fresh berries after removing the grilled fruit from the heat and covering for a few minutes to warm through.

Brandied Fruit

Red Pepper and Papaya Salsa

1 large red bell pepper, halved
1 large ripe papaya, peeled, seeded and finely diced
2 green onions, thinly sliced
3 tablespoons chopped fresh cilantro
2 to 3 tablespoons fresh lime juice
1 jalapeño pepper,* finely chopped

*Jalapeño peppers can sting and irritate the skin; wear rubber gloves when handling peppers and do not touch eyes. Wash hands after handling.

1. Grill bell pepper halves skin sides down on covered or uncovered grill over medium to hot coals 15 to 25 minutes or until skin is charred, without turning. Remove from grill and place in plastic bag until cool enough to handle, about 10 minutes.

2. Place papaya in medium bowl. Stir in onions, cilantro, 2 tablespoons lime juice and jalapeño. Remove bell pepper skins with paring knife and discard. Chop bell pepper and stir into papaya mixture. Add remaining 1 tablespoon lime juice, if desired. Serve chilled or at room temperature over grilled chicken.

Makes 6 servings

Variation: Vary this intriguing salsa by using a ripe mango or nectarines instead of a papaya. Basil and mint infuse the salsa with an even more tropical flavor. It is also great with grilled fish, chicken, clams, oysters or fajitas.

An average fire uses 3 to 4 pounds of charcoal.

Red Pepper and Papaya Salsa

Strawberry Blueberry Salsa

¾ **cup chopped strawberries**
⅓ **cup chopped blueberries**
2 **tablespoons chopped green bell pepper**
2 **tablespoons chopped carrot**
1 **tablespoon chopped onion**
2 **teaspoons cider vinegar**
1 **teaspoon minced jalapeño pepper***
⅛ **teaspoon ground ginger**

Jalapeño peppers can sting and irritate the skin; wear rubber gloves when handling peppers and do not touch eyes. Wash hands after handling.

Combine all ingredients in small bowl. Let stand 20 minutes to allow flavors to blend. Serve with grilled chicken, pork or fish. *Makes 4 servings*

Santa Fe Pineapple Salsa

2 **cups finely chopped DOLE® Fresh Pineapple**
1 **can (8 ounces) red, pinto or kidney beans, drained and rinsed**
1 **can (8¼ ounces) whole kernel corn, drained**
1 **cup chopped DOLE® Red or Green Bell Pepper**
½ **cup finely chopped DOLE® Red Onion**
2 **tablespoons chopped fresh cilantro**
1 **to 2 teaspoons seeded and chopped fresh jalapeño pepper**
½ **teaspoon grated lime peel**
2 **tablespoons lime juice**

• Combine pineapple, beans, corn, bell pepper, onion, cilantro, jalapeño, lime peel and juice in medium serving bowl. Cover and chill at least 30 minutes to allow flavors to blend. Serve with grilled salmon and asparagus. Garnish with grilled pineapple wedges, if desired.

• Salsa can also be served as a dip with tortilla chips or spooned over quesadillas or tacos. *Makes 10 servings*

Prep Time: 20 minutes
Chill Time: 30 minutes

Strawberry Blueberry Salsa

Calypso Grilled Pineapple

½ cup *French's®* Worcestershire Sauce
½ cup honey
½ cup (1 stick) butter or margarine
½ cup packed light brown sugar
½ cup dark rum
 1 pineapple, cut into 8 wedges and cored*
   Vanilla ice cream

You can substitute other fruits, such as halved peaches, nectarines or thick slices of mangoes, for the pineapple.

To prepare sauce, combine Worcestershire, honey, butter, sugar and rum in 3-quart saucepan. Bring to a full boil over medium-high heat, stirring often. Reduce heat to medium-low. Simmer 12 minutes or until sauce is slightly thickened, stirring often. Remove from heat; cool completely.

Brush pineapple wedges with some of the sauce. Place pineapple on oiled grid. Grill over hot coals 5 minutes or until glazed, turning and basting often with sauce. Serve pineapple with ice cream and remaining sauce. Garnish as desired. Refrigerate any leftover sauce.**   *Makes 8 servings (1½ cups sauce)*

**Leftover sauce may be reheated in microwave. Microwave and stir for 30 seconds at a time.*

Prep Time: 15 minutes
Cook Time: 15 minutes

Calypso Grilled Pineapple

Corn & Bean Salsa

⅓ cup olive oil
3 tablespoons *Frank's® RedHot®* Original Cayenne Pepper Sauce
3 tablespoons red wine vinegar
2 tablespoons minced fresh cilantro leaves
1 clove garlic, minced
½ teaspoon chili powder
¼ teaspoon salt
1 package (9 ounces) frozen corn, thawed and drained
1 can (16 ounces) black beans, drained and rinsed
1 large ripe tomato, chopped
2 green onions, thinly sliced

Whisk together oil, **Frank's RedHot** Sauce, vinegar, cilantro, garlic, chili powder and salt in large bowl until blended. Add corn, beans, tomato and onions; toss well to coat evenly. Cover and refrigerate 30 minutes before serving. Serve with grilled steak or hamburgers. *Makes 6 servings (about 4 cups salsa)*

Old-Fashioned Corn Relish

⅓ cup cider vinegar
2 tablespoons sugar
1 tablespoon cornstarch
3 tablespoons *French's® Classic Yellow®* Mustard
¼ teaspoon seasoned salt
1 package (9 ounces) frozen corn, thawed and drained
½ cup chopped celery
½ cup chopped red bell pepper
¼ cup finely chopped red onion
3 tablespoons sweet pickle relish

Combine vinegar, sugar and cornstarch in large microwave-safe bowl; mix well. Stir in mustard and salt. Microwave, uncovered, on HIGH 1 to 2 minutes or until thickened, stirring once. Add corn, celery, pepper, onion and pickle relish; toss well to coat evenly. Cover and refrigerate 30 minutes before serving. Serve as a relish on hamburgers or hot dogs, or serve with grilled meats. *Makes about 3 cups*

Top to bottom: Corn & Bean Salsa and Old-Fashioned Corn Relish

Premier Potato Salad

1½ **pounds small red potatoes, quartered**
⅓ **cup olive oil**
¼ **cup** *French's®* **Bold n' Spicy Brown Mustard or Classic Yellow®**
Mustard
3 **tablespoons lemon juice**
¼ **teaspoon black pepper**
1 **cup diagonally sliced celery**
1 **bell pepper (green, red or yellow) cut into strips**
2 **green onions, thinly sliced**
¼ **cup minced fresh parsley**

1. Cook potatoes, in enough salted boiling water to cover, 15 minutes or until slightly tender. Rinse with cold water and drain.

2. Combine oil, mustard, lemon juice and black pepper in large bowl. Add potatoes, celery, bell pepper, onions and parsley; toss well to coat evenly. Cover; refrigerate 1 hour before serving.   *Makes 8 servings*

Favorite Macaroni Salad

8 **ounces uncooked medium shell pasta**
⅓ **cup reduced-fat sour cream**
⅓ **cup reduced-fat mayonnaise**
⅓ **cup** *French's®* **Bold n' Spicy Brown Mustard**
1 **tablespoon cider vinegar**
3 **cups bite-sized fresh vegetables, such as tomatoes, peppers,**
carrots and celery
¼ **cup minced green onions**

1. Cook pasta according to package directions using shortest cooking time; rinse with cold water and drain.

2. Combine sour cream, mayonnaise, mustard and vinegar in large bowl. Add pasta, vegetables and green onions. Toss gently to coat evenly. Season to taste with salt and pepper. Cover; chill in refrigerator 30 minutes. Stir before serving.
Makes 6 (1-cup) servings

Top to bottom: Premier Potato Salad and Favorite Macaroni Salad

Acknowledgments

The publisher would like to thank the companies and organizations listed below for the use of their recipes and photographs in this publication.

American Lamb Council

Butterball® Turkey

Cherry Marketing Institute

Del Monte Corporation

Dole Food Company, Inc.

Filippo Berio® Olive Oil

Florida Department of Agriculture and Consumer Services, Bureau of Seafood and Aquaculture

The Golden Grain Company®

Hebrew National®

Heinz North America

The Hidden Valley® Food Products Company

Hillshire Farm®

The Kingsford® Products Co.

Lawry's® Foods

MASTERFOODS USA

McIlhenny Company (TABASCO® brand Pepper Sauce)

National Honey Board

National Pork Board

North Dakota Beef Commission

Reckitt Benckiser Inc.

The J.M. Smucker Company

Reprinted with permission of Sunkist Growers, Inc.

Unilever Bestfoods North America

Index

METRIC CONVERSION CHART

VOLUME MEASUREMENTS (dry)

$^1/_8$ teaspoon = 0.5 mL
$^1/_4$ teaspoon = 1 mL
$^1/_2$ teaspoon = 2 mL
$^3/_4$ teaspoon = 4 mL
1 teaspoon = 5 mL
1 tablespoon = 15 mL
2 tablespoons = 30 mL
$^1/_4$ cup = 60 mL
$^1/_3$ cup = 75 mL
$^1/_2$ cup = 125 mL
$^2/_3$ cup = 150 mL
$^3/_4$ cup = 175 mL
1 cup = 250 mL
2 cups = 1 pint = 500 mL
3 cups = 750 mL
4 cups = 1 quart = 1 L

VOLUME MEASUREMENTS (fluid)

1 fluid ounce (2 tablespoons) = 30 mL
4 fluid ounces ($^1/_2$ cup) = 125 mL
8 fluid ounces (1 cup) = 250 mL
12 fluid ounces (1$^1/_2$ cups) = 375 mL
16 fluid ounces (2 cups) = 500 mL

WEIGHTS (mass)

$^1/_2$ ounce = 15 g
1 ounce = 30 g
3 ounces = 90 g
4 ounces = 120 g
8 ounces = 225 g
10 ounces = 285 g
12 ounces = 360 g
16 ounces = 1 pound = 450 g

DIMENSIONS

$^1/_{16}$ inch = 2 mm
$^1/_8$ inch = 3 mm
$^1/_4$ inch = 6 mm
$^1/_2$ inch = 1.5 cm
$^3/_4$ inch = 2 cm
1 inch = 2.5 cm

OVEN TEMPERATURES

250°F = 120°C
275°F = 140°C
300°F = 150°C
325°F = 160°C
350°F = 180°C
375°F = 190°C
400°F = 200°C
425°F = 220°C
450°F = 230°C

BAKING PAN SIZES

Utensil	Size in Inches/Quarts	Metric Volume	Size in Centimeters
Baking or	8×8×2	2 L	20×20×5
Cake Pan	9×9×2	2.5 L	23×23×5
(square or	12×8×2	3 L	30×20×5
rectangular)	13×9×2	3.5 L	33×23×5
Loaf Pan	8×4×3	1.5 L	20×10×7
	9×5×3	2 L	23×13×7
Round Layer	8×1½	1.2 L	20×4
Cake Pan	9×1½	1.5 L	23×4
Pie Plate	8×1¼	750 mL	20×3
	9×1¼	1 L	23×3
Baking Dish	1 quart	1 L	—
or Casserole	1½ quart	1.5 L	—
	2 quart	2 L	—